KIND WORDS

Dr. Stephen Mansfield, Author and Business Leader

"It is rare that a book about the much-treated topic of leadership gives us so much that is new — new grids of understanding, new language that rivets meaning to our minds, even a new and refreshing level of transparency. Jack Nicholson and Rob Murray have offered leaders a valuable gift with their wisdom, their scholarship, and their compassion. This is just the type of book we need in our time."

Laura Fisher, PhD, Psychologist, Educator

"I've actively built a career around my passion to see individuals, groups and communities living with deepened levels of fullness and engaging the process of transformation. I have never read a book such as this. The transformational leadership framework and approach offered in this book is revolutionary. May we live our lives fully by integrating heart, soul, mind, and strength!"

Brooks Gibbs, PhD, Psychologist/Sociologist

"The Human Operating System concept is a fresh content carrier of ancient truths wrapped in an elegant user interface that makes reading easy and application even easier. Emerging young leaders, especially, have an opportunity to use the wisdom of this book to lay a foundation for a long, regret-free career. Those of us who are longer in the tooth can follow this book's counsel to recover and repair what we might have lost in the process of seeking great things for ourselves."

Chip Dodd, PhD, Author, Teacher, Mentor

"The Human Operating System offers its reader and doer a practical, purposeful, and passionate approach to living the full life of leadership, at home and at work. This work offers a plan of action that actually speaks to how we are created. It integrates heart, soul, mind and strength that develops the fullest, strongest leader, one who understands the power of excellence and compassion. Yes, the HOS is idealistic. However, if there were ever a time to renew and inhabit the great ideals of courage, compassion, the full life, love and leadership, now is the time."

Randy Tucker, President & CEO of Geodis (Retired October 2020)

"The Human Operating System gives any leader and organization the tools required to turn exhausting performance into exhilarating performance. The organization I was responsible for was exceptionally high performing in terms of Revenue, Earnings, and Cash Flow. At the end of each year we overachieved expectations and were completely exhausted and absent of celebration. That is because we operated mostly above the line. Then we found our heart and soul and we continued our exceptional performance with celebration and absent exhaustion. I invite you to operate below the line as well."

Bob Goff, New York Times Best Selling Author

"This book is not just an explanation, but a reminder about why we do what we do, the impact our lives can have in the world and an encouragement to carry on."

Amy Alexander, Licensed Marriage and Family Therapist
Executive Director, The Refuge Center for Counseling

"Self-awareness is perhaps the most critical quality of transformative leaders, and yet, too often it is not the most esteemed or discussed. This book changes that! The Human Operating System offers practical, insightful and empowering principles by endorsing a holistic approach to leadership that values authenticity, integration and community. When we are able to lead from this place we can access greater courage, clarity and creativity, and our product, relationships and culture are better for it."

Dr. Brad Smith, President, Bakke Graduate University
Chair, World Evangelical Alliance Global Institute of Leadership

"Business leaders are taught management as a human-disconnected science of efficiency and effectiveness. Yet true leadership requires a living dynamic of human motivation and passion. As a result, most managers face constant challenges without holistic tools for their success. In the book *The Human Operating System: Recovering the Heart and Soul of Your Leadership*, Jack Nicholson and Rob Murray provide a new perspective on organizational leadership and practical tools to help leaders reinvent themselves as whole leaders motivating the heart, soul, mind and strength of those they manage. Using the principles and tools in this book, organizational leaders will fnd a new enjoyment of their work as they energize their employees to new heights of motivation and connection to their work."

Dr. Doug Lucas, Founder and President of Team Expansion

"Wow. There's so much here. If Human Operating System were required reading for every MBA degree in North America, it would single-handedly restore the heart and soul of every leader, business, and organization on the continent. If you want to find meaning and peace while you labor and lead, read HOS. Then apply it. Then change the world."

Bill Wellons, Sr., Executive Director, The Fellowship Associates Leadership Residency, Little Rock, Arkansas

"The Human Operating System is a game changer for marketplace leaders. It's transformational! I experienced the inspiring insights and profound principles of this book firsthand when I met Jack 35 years ago. It launched a self-awareness journey in me that continues today. More than any other leadership book, *The Human Operating System* has given me a much greater understanding of the soul and design of my leadership. I use it regularly to impact the lives of the emerging leaders that I mentor. Buy a copy, read it carefully and integrate it personally. You will never regret doing so."

Matt Hangen, President and CEO at Water4

"At 34, I was tapped to become CEO of a then $6M international NGO with no executive experience. I had no idea then how important it was to be an integrated leader as I navigated difficult relationships, funding losses, and necessary acquisitions in my first year. The process laid out in HOS has been life-changing, marriage-enhancing, and personally liberating. Five years into the journey I am still a Spartan-spirited entrepreneur, but one now who knows how to build and appreciate a balanced team inside our mission and growth-driven organization."

Bob Westfall, Founder and CEO Westfall Gold & Author

"Speechless! Could be the most revolutionary business book of my lifetime. Full of empirical data, anecdotal evidence, and practical application. Follow these truths and principles and it could culminate in revolutionary transformational impact in your business, and personal life."

Barry White, Retired VP at Chick-fil-A Inc,
Husband, Father and Son

"Leadership is an incredible opportunity and gift that has been given to many, but a fully integrated leader is very difficult to identify in today's culture. Why is that? I have struggled as you might have on what a totally integrated leader looks like and how I can be the very best in the leadership roles I have been given at work and at home. Jack's and Rob's content will help you understand and execute what a fully integrated leader looks like and how it will help your business, your marriage and your decisions. It's hard work and this book is a great starting place. It is worth the effort!"

Rick Waggoner, Senior Vice President & Chief Development Officer, Convoy of Hope

"Very few books have content truly capable of transforming leaders. This is one of those books. Jack and Rob bring to light challenging perspectives that so clearly explain why many leaders struggle to thrive or burn out. I immediately saw myself in their stories of other leaders. At a practical level, the four quadrants theme throughout the book enhanced my understanding and gave me a path to application."

The Human Operating System

Recovering the Heart and Soul of Your Leadership

Jack Nicholson and Rob Murray

Telocity Media
Transformative Leadership Resources
Nashville, TN
www.transformedleader.com

Ordering Information: Quantity sales. Special discounts are available on quantity purchases by corporations, associations, and others. For details, contact the publisher at transformedleader.com.

Printed in the United States of America
ISBN Paperback: 9781735935218
ISBN Hardback: 9781735935201
www.transformedleader.com

First Edition

Dedicated to the leaders who are not yet living below the line.
You will be soon.

Are you ready?

CONTENTS

FOREWORD 1

INTRODUCTION 5
Installing Your New Operating System

1. LEARNING HOW TO BREATHE 17
Navigating the Polarity of Individual and Context

2. EMBODYING THE TRUE SELF 33
Integrating the Four Quadrants

3. FINDING YOUR FLOW 51
Engaging Your Unique Design and Contributions

4. WORKING BELOW THE LINE 75
Harnessing the Transformational Pathway of Change

5. STRENGTHENING THE CIRCLE 93
Nurturing Trust in Community

6. WHERE DO WE GO FROM HERE? 117
Building and Installing the Apps on the OS

END NOTES 137

FOREWORD

My first interaction with Jack Nicholson (no, not the actor) was on a phone call during my drive to the Des Moines, Iowa airport. I had attended a leadership meeting for the company where I had spent my career— Wells Fargo, one of the top five banks in America. I started in an entry-level role right out of college and had climbed the corporate ladder to a point that I had not thought possible as a young man. My career was humming along nicely, and I was seen as a "key leader" in the large organization I'd dedicated my life to.

It gets better. I married my college sweetheart, who is a brilliant healthcare provider and better than me in every possible way. We had three beautiful kids—a son and two daughters. We loved to travel and had been to places I didn't know existed when I was growing up in a small town in Nebraska. I was deeply involved in our community and serving as a leader at our church. To put it plainly, I was winning at life.

Yet, I was angry, discontent, often frustrated, easily irritated. Something just wasn't right. As I approached mid-life, it was clear that something needed to change. In that first conversation, Jack asked me what I thought the problem was. I responded by saying the bag of tricks that had gotten me this far just didn't seem to work anymore.

I'd devoted my life to a way of doing things—an operating system—that didn't work; I was clearly seeing the outcomes. I'd read everything I could get my hands on about marriage, parenting, personal growth, family systems, and leadership. I'd even gone down the path of studying brain science and attachment theory. I had more knowledge than I knew what to do with, yet little was changing. I was living my life entirely above the line. While everything looked great on the outside, I was headed toward a reckoning on the inside.

Jack and Rob took me on a journey that I could not have imagined. I've spent the last six years learning a whole new way to understand myself, the world around me, and what it takes to be the kind of partner, parent, and leader I have longed to be. From understanding my background and how it shaped me to discovering what it means to become a whole-hearted and integrated human being, a transformation had begun.

Many amazing resources are available for anyone who wants to improve their leadership—books, seminars, podcasts, and coaches galore. What they've missed is the foundational understanding of how humans were designed for transformation, and how that transformation can happen. Beginning to understand the reality of my Shadow-Self and the essence of my True-Self, opened up perspectives and possibilities I had never considered.

This began my journey toward transformational leadership. As my understanding of my True-Self grew, my ever-present irritability started to fade. By working through the four quadrants and understanding the importance of integrating all four of them, I'm not as tied to anger as I was once was. Learning to go "below the line" in my life has brought me to more contentment with myself and others. That sense that something wasn't right has been replaced with an expectant anticipation that I'm finally on the path where I belong.

Since my journey began, I've made a substantial career change. I left the relative comfort and security of an executive position at a large company to join the leadership team of a rapidly growing and dynamic smaller company. It's a risk I could not have taken before I understood the Human Operating System. At the time of this writing, I've spent two years in my current role; we've grown our business over 300% with no end in sight. Two years in a row, our company was voted as one of the best places to work in our city, and our team member turnover is nearly zero. Rather than leading only from Mind and Strength, we have worked to integrate Heart and Soul into our leadership, and the results are unquestionable.

The outcomes of this work in my professional life are only one piece. A couple of years ago, I had a conversation with my teenage son. He said to me, "Dad, I'm jealous of my little sisters. They're growing up with a much better dad than I did." He was spot-on.

The only thing that stings more than realizing you've let down the people you love the most is realizing it and doing nothing to change it. My son meant what he said to me as an encouragement—that he could see the change in me.

I'm still on the journey with much more work to do. And I'm excited that, with the publication of this book, you get to join me and others who have learned so much from Rob and Jack. This is your red pill or blue pill moment, my friend. You can continue to ignore that sense that things aren't quite right. Or you can anesthetize yourself with more—more stuff, more accolades, more success, and more accumulation. You can go all-in on the most recent leadership idea or the new way to do team-member development. Or you can choose to embrace a deeper understanding of the Human Operating System and install it in your life. It won't be easy, but it is the path to true human flourishing—for you, the people you love, and the people you lead.

Tony Julianelle
Father, Husband, Friend
CEO, Atlas Real Estate
Denver, CO

INTRODUCTION

Installing Your New Operating System

When was the last time you woke up and thought about the operating system on your phone or computer? Probably not lately. We know there is an operating system, and we know that periodically we get asked to update or upgrade the OS on our electronic devices so that they will, in some mysterious way, work better. But our interest in operating systems generally stops there.

It's like the construction materials used to build the house you live in. Unless you're a contractor or hobbyist, your interest is confined to the end product—the house and its furnishings, not the two-by-fours underneath the drywall. Unless you're a computer programmer, you're probably not terribly curious about the language hiding behind the curtain of code and technology. Most of us want to know only one thing: *Does it work?*

We want to know that when we hit the power button, the screen will light up, there will be an instant connection to the internet gods, and we'll be able to check the weather, stock prices, calendar, and email in the blink of an eye. For most of us, technology is about getting immediate access to the information and interaction we need to run our lives a little more smoothly and a little more quickly.

Even the applications themselves may intrigue us momentarily with clever names and pretty images, but within seconds, it's all about what they do for us. If they don't improve the quality of our lives pretty fast, we simply delete them and move on to the next. Apps are there to help us express, interact, and connect as we engage life with friends, colleagues, and the world at large. *It's the connection we're really after.*

Even though few of us care directly about the operating systems we use, they matter enormously. If the OS fails, everything built on top of it fails. If the OS runs out of resources, all our apps slow to a crawl and become an impediment to our lives rather than an aid to them. In addition, not every operating system is created equal; put a group of Mac and PC users together in a room, and a colorful dialog will quickly emerge on that very point.

We can say with confidence that our electronic devices—and all the functions they allow—rise or fall on the integrity of the operating system underneath. *We can also say with confidence that our personal and professional lives rise or fall on the integrity of the "operating system" within us.* Programmers go to great lengths to hide the complexity of code behind an engaging interface that is beautiful and intuitive. And that is the purpose of this book: to simplify the most complex and crucial elements of our lives so we can operate at our fullest capacity of purpose, enjoyment, and harmony with others.

SIMPLICITY ON THE OTHER SIDE OF COMPLEXITY

The Human Operating System (HOS) is a powerful metaphor for describing the ultimate realities of how people, leaders, and relational systems function. The archetypal model we're going to describe here will serve as a foundational set of principles and processes that can be installed in your conscious awareness to empower your effectiveness in all dimensions of life. We invite you to explore a way of looking at a reality that can holistically undergird any strategic initiative that a leader, team, or organization might take. The HOS offers a common language, framework, and interface for leaders who want to move beyond former limitations into bold new levels of growth and strength.

Too many of today's business processes are overly complicated, and it's like teaching computer code to users who will never be software engineers. It's impractical and uninspiring to deal with complexity when we long for the elegance of simplicity. As is attributed to the brilliant Renaissance artist Leonardo da Vinci, "Simplicity is the ultimate sophistication."

We get to observe this truth in something as common as a corporate mission statement that emerges from an elaborate envisioning and consulting process. Once that verbiage grows beyond a sentence or so, no one can remember it, and at that point, people cease to care. But a powerful, concise mission statement that can stick in the mind as a fundamental principle—this provides a focus, a bearing that can be constantly applied and reinforced in daily activities. That kind of simplicity on the other side of complexity can fuel an entire enterprise.

The HOS is a powerful force that can guide leadership teams to wisely engage structural and systemic problems. It is a simple, elegant way to understand complex issues and the relational dynamics that motivate organizations to be healthy and productive. If a fundamental principle is going to be broadly useful, it must be simple and memorable. This is our goal, and we welcome you to explore this model with an open heart and mind as we guide you through these illuminating ideas.

A CRISIS OF CULTURE

Needless complexity is not the only threat to the modern leadership culture, is it? The lack of a healthy operating system has infected the contemporary workplace like a virus, and as a result, corporate "apps" are failing at epic rates. The legacy of broken operating systems across the corporate landscape is apparent: low morale, low satisfaction, high conflict, high turnover.

Many leaders leverage their intelligence, competence, and discipline into positions of great influence only to pay the price as their efforts begin to break down under overwhelming demands. Because half their human system is offline, it lacks the bandwidth to address the breadth of life. We'll be addressing the other half shortly, but when the system can't support the demand, the only solution is to disengage and detach.

Most frequently, what internal bandwidth is available to us gets allocated toward productivity—getting stuff done. This is where we get rewarded in most leadership environments, leaving relationships to be perpetually deferred. In this environment we tend to be emotionally unavailable to spouses, children, friends, and even colleagues, leading to a loss of joy and meaning in the absence of intimacy.

Burnout, divorce, addiction, depression, anxiety: the natural consequences of HOS failure are prevalent. On the organizational side, management teams experience fragmentation, competition, and conflict both in personal and communal dimensions. We are paying a high price for such systemic collapse, and the cost shows up on the bottom line of financial statements, not to mention the bottom line of the human experience.

A 2016 study by global analytics giant McKinsey & Company noted that only 11 percent of executives are satisfied with their leadership programs.[1] This sobering reality has motivated us even more to search out for leadership solutions, consultants, and approaches in our own areas of influence that could help collectively contribute with others to turn this tide. We believe there is a desire in the marketplace for innovative change, drawing the best from our current models, while also recovering and renewing the parts and pieces that may have been under-prioritized along the way.

STANDING AT THE CROSSROADS

This systemic brokenness isn't just academic for us; we both have very up-close-and-personal stories about wrestling with these forces. I (Rob) was thirty-six years old when my wife walked into the room one day and asked if we could talk.

Uh-oh. This can't be good, I thought, but I faked calm and answered, "Sure."

Sitting down on the edge of the bed, Natalie looked at me earnestly. "Rob, you're a great dad to our four kids and a good husband to me. You're working so hard to take care of us—building your business, finishing your Master's Degree. You provide well, you love us, you're totally committed to us."

I nodded cautiously, hearing a "but" coming.

"But . . . I miss you. I want more of you. I'm lonely. So often you're here physically, but you're not really here. Do you think there could be another way for us to do life that would include me getting my husband back?"

A hundred protests died on my lips as the weight of her words crashed in on me. In a moment of absolute clarity, I knew there was real truth here. As a South African, my genetic instinct for survival comes with a built-in message: Get busy and get it done. As a result, I was running on fumes, chasing the dream of success and security. Going out into the world to fight for a life, yet never coming home to actually live it. The mental and emotional exhaustion had about crushed me, and I was starting to resent climbing that ladder. It was costing me my family; it was costing me my soul. Something had to give.

Days later, I walked into a counselor's office with some trepidation. Jeff asked why I was there, and I began to unpack my story. I told him about the conversation with my wife and all that led up to it, sprinkling in my self-diagnoses in case he needed some help with that. He didn't.

Jeff was compassionate but direct. "You've cracked open the lid to your sewer drain, Rob, and you're starting to see a few fragments that you've flushed down there. But you have no idea the parts of your unreconciled past that you have tried to bury. If you're going to reclaim your heart and find the life you long for, it's going to be a challenging journey."

He leaned back and paused. "You've come to this place for a reason, and now you have a decision to make. You can slap that lid closed, muster up some fresh determination, and power through a couple of more years. You're young and driven; you can reengage your coping mechanisms to gut it out for a few more laps. Or you can open the lid wider, climb down into the sewer drain, and sort through all the discarded parts of your heart and soul until you come out the other end. You can do it now, or you can do it years from now. It's up to you."

Taken aback, I felt like the Tin Man in *The Wizard of Oz*; I had most certainly lost heart. Looking down, I began to realize how many of my body parts had been replaced with metal, trading the human parts to become more efficient, more powerful, more unfeeling. The world had demanded better, faster, and stronger from me. Who had I even become? I scarcely recognized the hard shell.

But the inner voice was insistent. *No, that's a terrible idea, Jeff. Um, we're not opening any sewer drains. I was hoping to pay for some tips on becoming a better husband so I could go home and win this thing! Maybe I was not clear.* But the next voice gripped me like a vise. *What if I do nothing, only to cycle back in a couple of years—and Natalie and the kids aren't here anymore?* I had to admit that possibility. Her question to me was definitely a cry for connection, a plea for change. Could I really ignore that? The cost would only increase.

Jeff could see my inner turmoil as I negotiated furiously with myself. His words were compassionate but direct. "I understand, really. It's okay. What I am suggesting is a lot. Why not go take another lap, and I'll see you in a few years?"

I knew he was right, but I was terrified of opening the lid. I continued to sit there deliberating. After a couple of moments, he leaned in close and gently whispered, "I'll go with you. I'll go with you."

And he did. With Jeff's encouragement and Natalie's support, I began my personal journey for authenticity, whole-heartedness, and transformation. It was one of the most important decisions of my life.

You've probably read the onslaught of popular business books, and maybe you, too, have exhausted yourself trying to follow their advice. *Crush it, kill it, drag it home, repeat!* The message is usually some form of, "You're going to be amazing if you'll just work smarter and harder using our special sauce."

This is not that.

The HOS is as old as humanity. We didn't invent it. We've just spent a lot of years trying to understand it and communicate it in ways that are transformative. And frankly, we've had to learn most of it the hard way. Fortunately, what we're learning is changing our lives and the lives of organizational leaders across the country.

HUMANIZING THE LEADERSHIP JOURNEY

There are lots of "Tin Men" in the corporate race, those who feel like they've traded their humanity for something more machine-like. Hijacked by the relentless pursuit of profit at the expense of meaning, many we've talked with feel chewed up and spit out, over-worked, under-appreciated, and unfulfilled.

This organizational brokenness is exacerbated by the cultural trend of "instant impatience." Dozens of studies have concluded that emergent generations are becoming less and less willing to wait patiently for anything, including the investment needed for lasting qualitative growth.[2] Instant gratification is simply too appealing, even if it's an illusion. The pretense of a fast growth is preferable to the reality of a slow growth.

We all know that an advertisement has only seconds to reach someone's attention and establish a connection before getting lost in the noise of competing voices. This dynamic panders to glitzy but shallow at the expense of honest and substantial. The truth is, meaningful and enduring development—whether in individuals or enterprises—takes time. Strong leaders can't be microwaved. The attempt merely generates more "Tin Men." There are no shortcuts to sustainable health, which is why the HOS holds such merit for long-term cultivation of culture.

Some organizations and leadership consultants have embraced a developmental mindset for their executive leaders and management teams. Others, however, are limited in their enthusiasm for this type of work and consider it to be a necessary line item in the budget, and other decision makers have failed to engage an intentional leadership strategy altogether for varying reasons. We gain encouragement and motivation from those leaders who are committed to a pathway of deepening themselves and those around them. How can we dream and collaborate with enlightened leaders to bring more humanity into the world of commerce?

At the same time that the public is losing confidence in corporations and government, people are increasingly craving meaning, purpose, and community. They want to work hard, but they want their work to have a soul—and to believe that in some sense and some form, their work is making the world better. There's a hunger for vision and passion—to belong to something bigger than ourselves, something that matters. We want more respect and trust, more collaboration and empowerment. Is this too much to ask? We think not. We believe that American business is being invited into a revolution, something that will be good for the employee, good for the stakeholder, and good for the world.

Another way of saying it is that the time and priorities of executive leadership can become too narrowly focused upon *products* and *profits* at the expense of *people* and *purpose.* We are entering a purpose-driven economy, where consumers will increasingly begin to demand social meaning in their purchasing. We've seen the innovators move in this direction, and the early adoption trend is strong. If this speaks to something deep in you, let's learn together how to humanize the leadership journey.

HITTING THE WALL

I (Jack) would like to share a turning point from my leadership journey that will hopefully encourage those of you who are in the fog of liminal space. "Liminal" is Latin for *threshold,* and crossing thresholds of personal and professional leadership is a significant theme in this book.

Looking back over a long life, I have to acknowledge that my childhood was rough. An emotionally distant father and an abusive mother left me scrambling to find my way in the world, and without realizing it, I did what a lot of wounded men do: attempt to find a sense of belonging and personal worth through achievement and external validation. But my coping strategy wasn't working.

I chose a small Christian college and made my way through a series of non-profit leadership roles with reasonable amounts of success. But a disheartening divorce in my thirties followed by a disappointing departure from ministry leadership left me reeling and disoriented. All of the emptiness and insecurity of my childhood seemed to return with a vengeance as I searched for a completely new career track. Without a marriage, without money, lacking a plan, and lacking confidence, it was a dark and lonely time. I had hit the wall.

"How do you feel about selling fire extinguishers?"

I looked at my friend with a blank expression. Frank was an experienced salesman in industrial products, and knowing that I needed a job, he asked me if I'd like to help him launch a new product line. If the offer had felt like pity, I would have quickly refused. Instead, I felt something radically different. Something so different I didn't really have a name for it, but now I would call it *belief*. Frank saw something in me that I could not yet see in myself. I felt the power of his confidence in me, and that was enough to give me the courage to cross this threshold.

The sales presentation for the extinguisher was dramatic. I would pour lighter fluid on my briefcase and set it on fire! Once the flames leapt about three feet in the air and the buyers stepped back wide-eyed, I would give it a blast with the halon gas. As the fire vanished instantly, the effect was magical, and I sold a lot of extinguishers. The high point, literally, came at a large bus complex at the Metropolitan Transit Authority, where the flames got high enough to set off the fire alarm and bring in the fire department. I let Frank talk to the fire marshal, while I quietly hung around in the back of the crowd. We toned it down a little after that.

While my sales experience was growing, something more quiet and profound was taking place on the inside. I was running a demo at the University of Cincinnati when I first became aware of it: I could see myself making the presentation, while being engaged in the process at the same time. I suddenly felt solid, present, and confident in who I was as a man, and from that moment on, I no longer needed to perform for my worth.

I'm not a young man any longer, and I can attest that the convoluted path of life and leadership has the potential to serve us immensely if we pay attention. Both the places of suffering and the places of breakthrough contain a formative invitation to our true selves and those who become students of their own growth accumulate wisdom they can then offer to others. Through the years, I have often wondered, *How did I get here?* My leadership journey is not one that I could have planned for or made happen through the force of my will. It is truly a mystery, but I know that hitting the wall was part of that journey, and learning to trust my true self was the critical turning point.

Helping leaders experience deep change and transformation is now my life's calling: to be a source of sage counsel to those who are navigating the confusing course of their personal and professional journey. Looking back on that long, difficult season in my life, I can see how some of the truths we are sharing in this book were seeded in my soul at that time, laying a foundation for my life and career to come. In the midst of my liminal space, the power of the HOS was starting to come online for the first time, and if you can identify with hitting the wall, I welcome you onto a path that will transform your life.

At our organization, Transformed Leader, we have been pioneering the HOS for years, and we have seen the results—both qualitative and quantitative—of replacing broken systems with those that work. We have observed firsthand the transformational impact of the HOS on leaders at the peak of commerce. We have seen men and women move from burnt-out to fired-up. We have supported these leaders on their journeys to reclaim their soul, their marriage, and their career. Organizational cultures have pivoted from sputtering to rebirth, and so can yours. Take a look at Brad's story.

THE COLLECTIVE GLOBAL STORY

Brad Stinson was on his way up the corporate ladder, having invested fourteen years at two Fortune 500 companies. He was an eager and attentive learner—watching, reading, and absorbing the best skills he could find in the rarified air of leadership development. But he was losing traction in the competitive jungle when he met us.

Using the HOS, I (Jack) walked him through the reasons he felt so driven to prove himself to others and to himself. Brad was in touch with the fierce compulsion to achieve, but he didn't understand where it was coming from and why it was hurting him and those he loved. His feelings of inadequacy were terrifying and beginning to undermine his success. I invited him into an experiential learning process with the quadrants of reality, where he could look at himself—and even give advice to himself—from four different perspectives. It was an emotional experience that took Brad back to a message he had received twenty-five years earlier from his grandfather, and once that false belief was lifted, everything changed.

As a result of embracing his full humanity through the HOS, Brad realized that his purpose in life wasn't to climb his own ladder but to help others climb theirs, while using this powerful tool. He began to integrate these principles into his own coaching and consulting company called The Collective Global, where he and his colleagues now take other leaders through parts of the HOS and regularly receive comments like, "In my entire twenty-five-year career, nothing compares to the experience we had with you." The simplicity and potency of the HOS changed the course and quality of Brad's leadership and is now being multiplied in the lives of scores of new companies.

In the pages that follow, we will guide you through an ancient, timeless paradigm that has the potential to retool your life and your leadership so that you, too, can be whole-hearted again. We have walked this road ourselves. Come with us on a journey to uncover the four dimensions of the HOS system, to integrate them fully into your life, and to walk a transformational pathway into your destiny. Here's a preview of where we're headed—each chapter will reveal one of the five critical principles for understanding and applying the HOS in your own growth as a human and a leader.

FIVE CRITICAL PRINCIPLES OF THE HOS

- Leadership growth and organizational development are interdependent.
- Leadership growth requires the integration of Heart, Soul, Mind, and Strength.
- Leadership growth is fueled by harnessing your unique design and flow.
- Leadership growth is catalyzed by a transformational pathway of change.
- Leadership growth deepens within relationships of trust.

Friend, this is a time for courage. For bold moves and smart risks. It's time to let go of the numbing comfort and predictability of the status quo and reach for more. *There is more!* So, let's get started on understanding the magical interplay between your personal growth and your organizational development.

REFLECTION QUESTIONS

1. *What has your experience been with the pervasive dehumanization of the business world?*

2. *How would you describe a personal or professional crisis that you have experienced, perhaps similar to* Rob *and Jack?*

3. *What are the symptoms of OS-failure, like burnout, marriage problems, addiction, depression, apathy, or anxiety, that you might be experiencing now?*

4. *What would motivate you to install a new, healthier operating system in your personal and professional leadership?*

1

LEARNING HOW TO BREATHE

Navigating the Polarity of Individual and Context

Danny was weary. Weary with trying to live up to the expectations of leadership thrust upon him in his organizational role in Argentina. Despite his best intentions and diligence, the results just weren't there, and his identity had taken a humbling shot to the chest. Along with his confidence. It wasn't working anymore, and Danny was scrambling for an honorable escape.

His exit strategy centered around finding a safer role back in the States, so when the opportunity arose, he made the leap to become executive director of a small nonprofit. Bolstering his image with a new master's degree and book publication, he tried to leave the deep lingering feelings of failure in the rearview mirror. Image management had become a full-time job.

Underneath the façade of achievement, his insecurity invaded his other roles as well. Life just doesn't compartmentalize as neatly as he sometimes wished. In his more honest moments, he had to admit that his engagement as a husband and father had taken a hit, along with his vocational confidence. He had started living small; small and safe became the over-riding objective. But an encounter with us in a leadership cohort changed all that.

The eighth workshop exposed the long-term message of shame that had sabotaged his leadership, both at home and at work. Honestly, it had undermined his very sense of self. But in that final session, he was able to name his enemy and step beyond all his clever defenses toward his true self. It was an emotional but absolutely liberating transition, and the results from that inner shift started multiplying exponentially.

He found new affection for his wife, fresh commitment to his three sons, and in less than two weeks, a prominent new leadership position in a company that tapped his fuller capacity and passion. Experiencing the HOS had been a game-changer and it continues to sustain his growth as a man and a leader. Danny's story illustrates HOS Principle #1: *Leadership growth and organizational development are interdependent.*

Nothing happens in a vacuum. Our operating system, whether healthy or dysfunctional, directs the course of our humanity and the context in which we live, love, and work. The "apps" of life can only be as healthy as the system that supports them. Danny's story highlights the intrinsic connection between what happens to us internally and what happens to us externally. There is no separating our development—or impediments to our development—as individuals and as leaders. These two dynamics function as a polarity: the individual on one end and context or environment on the other.

It's like breathing. We must both breathe in and breathe out. There is a fundamental interrelatedness between the *in* and the *out*; both are essential. If we polarize—stop at either end—we die. That rhythm of inflow and outflow is what sustains life at an organic level. Our mission, both in this book and in our organization, Transformed Leader, is to help people and companies learn how to breathe, better and deeper. In this chapter, we want to explore how and why the two poles are so dependent upon one another.

Life continually unfolds in and around us. We are growing, developing, and changing all the time. Some of this growth and development happens naturally; other parts can only happen *intentionally*, and those are the parts we'll be focusing upon. By working at the intersection of leadership growth and organizational development, we are able to leverage this complex and interactive process that we call the Human Polarity. This approach has radically impacted our work and supercharges the potential for strengthening the whole human ecosystem.

BALANCE AND IMBALANCE

In Figure 1.1, you'll see a simple image that represents the mutual dependency of the Human Polarity.

Figure 1.1

In a healthy polarity balance, both sides of the equation—the leader and the organization—get a proportional amount of attention and resource, resulting in sustainable growth on both poles. When leaders can be generative on both personal and professional dimensions, they are growing and developing in both places simultaneously. Growth on each side informs and empowers the other. The individual movement and organizational movement complement and synergize one another.

Let's go back to Danny's story. In his diminished capacity early in the story, both poles—his individual health and his leadership health—suffered. One influenced the other, and those influences were *largely negative*. After he was able to pivot by doing his inner work with the Human OS, both poles began to flourish. One influenced the other, and those influences were largely positive.

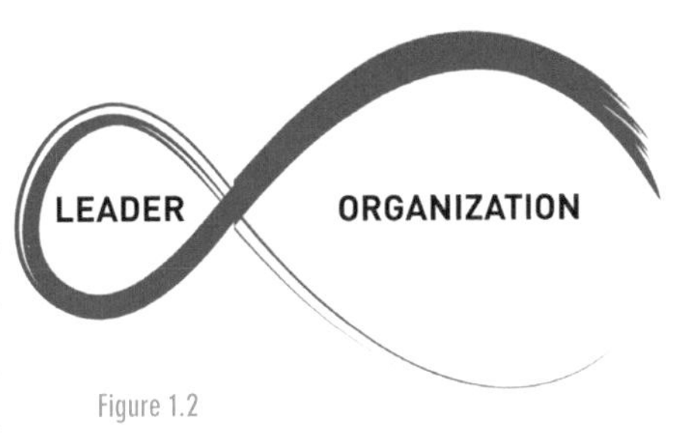

Figure 1.2

When the Human-System Polarity begins to unravel, however, it usually begins on one side or the other before the dysfunction spreads to the other side. In Figures 1.2 and 1.3, you'll see two images that represent the potential imbalances we can experience. In 1.2, the challenges or opportunities at work dwarf the reserves of the individual, generating a steady drain of energy and function. The system suffers until balance can be restored, either by dialing down the work demands or by dialing up the individual resources through some form of growth and development. Figure 1.3 shows the opposite possibility: the individual's capacity far exceeds what is being asked of him or her in the organization, leading perhaps to equal degrees of frustration as the first scenario and an equal need for re-balancing the equation.

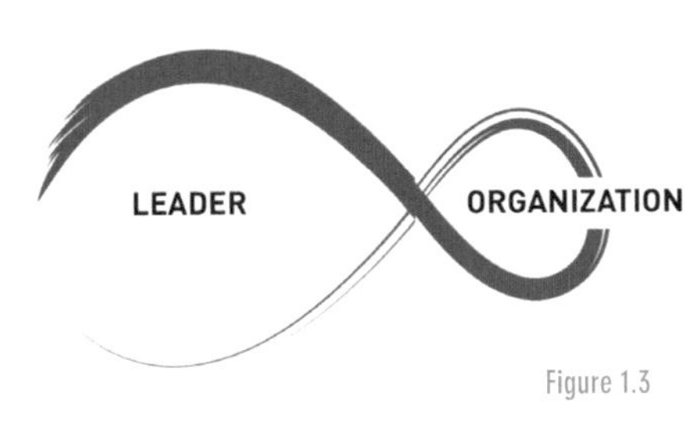

Figure 1.3

There are many nuances of these scenarios, of course, and the balance ratios tend to shift over time, depending generally on the rate of change and innovation in the organization and sometimes in the rate of personal development in the individual. Balance is almost never perfect, so it's important to develop an observation mechanism to evaluate these forces on a regular basis.

Let's work with this idea a little further.

There are myriads of circumstances that could fuel these particular imbalances. Consider these potential scenarios:

- Your company gets bought out and, overnight, a new management team shows up. Your leadership sphere could be upsized or down sized quite suddenly.
- There is a death in your immediate family, and equally suddenly, your emotional reserves are half their normal capacity.
- You get a promotion to a new level of leadership, and your staff and responsibilities double.
- You take a sabbatical for new schooling and return to work with a whole new set of skills, expertise, and vision.
- New competition emerges in your industry, and market share drops dramatically. The executive team responds by cutting budgets and staffing, leaving you to do more with less.

The combinations of factors like these are endless, and perhaps you've experienced one or two personally. Maybe you're experiencing one such imbalance right now and are trying to navigate your way through it. Be encouraged—we're here to supply language and perspective that will help you right-size the equation faster.

It's also worth noting that the balanced polarity represented in Figure 1.1 can either be healthy or unhealthy. The healthy version is that your resources and talents are being applied to the needs of the organization in ways that are satisfying and sustainable. One unhealthy version is that organizational demand has leapt forward (1.2), and you have responded by accessing greater capacity, yet your outflow is unsustainable. You are hyperventilating, and it's just a matter of time before emotional cardiac arrest.

The other unhealthy version of balance is that your work demands have lessened (1.3), yet for purposes of security or resistance to change, you have simply dumbed down your outflow. Now you're bored and falling asleep at the job. Although this scenario is less overtly stressful, it's still a slow-motion tragedy unfolding. In the first case, you've lost sustainability; in the second case, you've lost satisfaction. Neither of these "balances" produces meaningful growth, either personally or professionally. A healthy Human Polarity will match the true capacity of the leader to the demands of the context. Breathing in, breathing out, without either hyperventilating or falling asleep.

Leaders who actively cultivate both poles hold the best odds for finding this polarity synergy. Plus, leaders who are committed to their growth and integration have a compounding influence on the transformation of their organizations. And as organizations expand and come into their prime, they need leaders with increasing capacity, depth of character, and competency.

THE CORE COMPETENCIES OF EXECUTIVE LEADERSHIP

Owners, CEOs, and executive teams carry the weight of responsibility for the success of their business enterprises. We all know this. And to do this well, they must rise to the challenge of cultivating a balanced Human Polarity. One helpful framework for managing both poles is to look at the opportunities resident within the six core competencies of executive leadership:

1. *Developing Leaders*

High-capacity leadership must be recruited, developed, and empowered at all levels of an organization to keep a business enterprise in its prime. This is an ongoing need that has no one-time solution; it calls for a systematic process to manage this strategic need for the life of the organization. And what we're going to explore within the context of these core competencies is the dynamic interaction between both poles: individual and context.

Leadership development is dependent upon motivation. Growth is generally a choice, other than the rare exception when an adapt-or-die scenario is thrust upon us. Insightful leaders recognize where their resources are running too thin and where they need to invest in enlarging their professional skill set. Motivated leaders take action toward that goal, whether supported by the organization or not.

When a leader intentionally engages development of this pole—individual capacity—organic growth is the natural byproduct, and the benefits of that growth are felt across the spectrum of that person's life, as we saw in Danny's story. His narrative demonstrates the truth that personal growth impacted his marriage, his parenting, and his work life with transformational benefits. So, the correlation between the growth of the individual and growth in the organization is compelling. And it works in the other direction as well.

Organizational development builds the container that holds all the individual leaders within it. Smart organizations continually invest in structures that allow their leaders to work together effectively: there is both a systemic dimension to this development and a cultural dimension to it. Culture is the collection of values, norms, and processes that either facilitate or hinder healthy function, while systems are meant to undergird the culture to channel that energy forward. When an organization invests in its growth both structurally and culturally, it necessarily impacts the individual.

Wise growth in the enterprise sets an expectation for growth in the individual and also helps the individual find his or her right seat on the bus. Healthy, growing organizations make development of its individuals easily accessible within a culture that values growth across character, competency, and chemistry. In this way, the core competency of developing leaders becomes, not just a practical need to be met, but a powerful means of building corporate culture and fueling accomplishment of the mission itself.

2. *Building Teams*

Great teamwork is essential for success and it only takes one extraordinary leadership team to change the culture and activate the leader-organizational polarity. The interplay between individual and context on teams is managed organically within emotionally intelligent cultures and managed mechanically (as in poorly) within other more dysfunctional cultures. We will look into that spectrum later in the chapter.

The individual who wishes to operate within a team is responsible for developing and managing the particular skills, attitudes, and processes for healthy interaction. Self-knowledge and good communication, enthusiastic advocacy and deferring humility, the ability to challenge and the ability to encourage—all these and many more are collectively described as emotional intelligence. The individual leader who cultivates such intelligence and regularly implements these skills will empower the teams they participate in, at home and at work.

The organization that wishes to experience the unique synergy of effective teams will intentionally nurture a culture that values these relational dynamics. This is in contrast, of course, to organizational cultures that squelch honest dialog, risk-taking, and innovation. But organizations that reinforce and reward emotional intelligence create an environment that encourages the individual to grow in that direction. Health in one tends toward health in the other, and conversely, dysfunction in one tends toward dysfunction in the other, which is one reason culture-management is the top priority of great leaders.

3. Leading Change

Leading people through constructive paths of change accelerates the growth, development, and profitability of the enterprise. Becoming a skillful change agent within an organization is neither automatic nor easy. Leading change is a competency that takes intentionality and commitment. Let's look at how the polarity interrelationship works in this competency.

Individuals fall along a continuum of change resistance—to change tolerance—to change enthusiasm, and this posture in relation to change is influenced by a number of factors: personality, mission resonance, personal history, and emotional resiliency to name a few. Leaders who understand the necessity of change, who have cultivated a comfort with change, and who have learned how to implement constructive change strategies are those who can use their influence to help organizations adapt and grow. This capacity to lead organizational change is generally forged in the crucible of personal change. Those who resist personal change can rarely instigate and guide it when change is required of the organization.

Organizations have a life of their own; the culture of the group is determined by the amalgam of those individuals with influence. So, organizations as a whole develop a relationship with change that can be either positive or negative. Anxiety and resistance show up in all the "Here we go again" comments and eye-rolls that run like a virus through a company; alternatively, companies that actively foster a culture of creativity and innovation have learned how to ride the energy generated by change.

You can see how emotional resiliency affects both individuals and the groups they lead, and how each side of this polarity sparks and pushes the other. The individual's relationship with change bleeds into the executive team, and the executive team's atmosphere affects (or infects) the individuals. The two sides are organically connected.

4. *Transforming Conflict*

Conflict is inevitable in the human community, but how we respond to conflict separates healthy leaders and cultures from unhealthy ones. Managing conflict well is a skill set that smart leaders develop in order to transform explosive situations into positive outcomes and organizational energy. Interpersonal conflict is an invitation into learning, but it takes both individual and organizational savvy to harness the opportunity lest it be wasted in hostility and disunity.

The emotional energy behind conflict operates on at least three planes: *individual, relational,* and *group*. Individuals respond internally and instinctively to conflict in one of three ways: aggression, withdrawal, or acquiescence. Or more commonly known as *fight, flight,* or *freeze*. The relational dimension pits two individuals' conflict strategies against one another in a variety of potential combinations, and the group dimension often multiplies these dynamics throughout an entire room of people. Thus, the polarity of leader and context.

At Transformed Leader, we offer a variety of experiential workshops designed for individuals and teams to deepen their capacity, connection, character, and competence in leadership. In particular, we love a process called "Clearing the Charge," which leads individuals to clarify, own, and release emotional energy by taking responsibility for the intensity of their feelings. In this process, an emotional charge is broken down into its critical parts and then communicated to the person caught in the charge so that the relational tension is resolved in a healthy way. Through this and other strategies, interpersonal conflict can be harnessed and transformed into positive organizational energy.

5. *Fostering Innovation*

Rapid social, cultural, and technological changes require constant innovation for a business enterprise to adapt and survive, and this skill is intimately connected to the competency of leading change we just discussed. Again, we will briefly describe the polarity opportunity.

Innovation in the individual describes the intersection between a person's creative problem-solving ability and a person's comfort with deconstructing existing processes. And this capacity also runs along a continuum of degrees. One leader with this strength can catalyze the potential of a group in ways that make or break an enterprise, which may prompt that leader to, in turn, create a culture of creativity and innovation in the team or organization at large.

Innovation in the organization can run the reverse course and draw out the innovative potential of the individual. Seeds of creative change may lie dormant for decades within a leader—or even actively suppressed—until the corporate winds change, allowing for and even seeking out new possibilities. Growth in one tends to call forth growth in the other; paralysis in one tends to reinforce paralysis in the other.

It's important to note that the enemy of innovation and creativity for many leaders is the fear of failure and the need for survival. You can't ask leaders to risk innovating, while simultaneously threatening them with punishment should they fail. When failure is not an option, you're left playing it safe and innovation is the casualty.

6. *Leaving a Legacy*

True leadership must define and execute a compelling vision and strategy that makes a vital contribution to the future value of the business. Short-sightedness in a company can be lethal. We don't have space here to unpack the full generative potential of this core competency, but the ability to forego immediate gratification on an organizational level in order to lay the groundwork for inter-generational success is a rare and beautiful commodity.

The individual who cannot only forecast opportunities ten, twenty, or even fifty years ahead, but also evaluate that potential in terms of social value (which is not always measured in dollars) is a leader who can shape the trajectory of the future and, dare we say, change the world. That is some serious Human Polarity at work.

The organization that can forge a legacy-focused identity is one that has the potential to become the best version of itself. And when that identity is stewarded and protected by the daily decisions of its leaders, it seeps into the very air of organizational life, breathing new life into the lungs of its individual members and inviting them to live more meaningful lives.

CULTURE MANAGEMENT

Throughout our conversation of these six core competencies, the scarlet thread running along the organizational pole is a substance we can only call culture. This term gets a lot of lip service in the leadership industry, and it should. It's that important. But it also deserves an investment of substance. Why? *Because culture trumps vision every day of the week.*

We said earlier that culture is the collection of values, norms, and processes that define a group and either facilitate or hinder healthy function. Culture is unseen but felt keenly. It includes things like openness to new ideas, freedom to disagree respectfully, comfort levels with emotion, speed of change, how conflict is managed, and many more. These values and expectations form the container for all interaction and decision-making within the organization. They influence absolutely everything, yet they are rarely talked about openly or even overtly chosen. They simply appear from those with the most influence and are then reinforced with reward and punishment.

Any leader or enterprise that wishes to effectively manage the Human Polarity must come to terms with existing culture and then be willing and able to modify that culture if they wish to establish a healthy polarity that encourages growth on both poles, which is why this maxim also bears repeating: culture-management is the top priority of great leaders.

UNIVERSAL POLARITIES

In addition to grappling with cultural issues, leaders must also cultivate an eye for making critical decisions regarding the endless stream of problems that cross their desks, and the critical decision looks like this: *Is this challenge a problem to be solved or a polarity to be managed?*[3]

Problems to be solved are singular in nature—they rise once, invite a solution, and then disappear. If they rise regularly but are still solvable, they invite making a policy, which is nothing more than a consistent solution to a consistent challenge. But polarities are different: polarities are never solved; they can only be managed. Like breathing, polarities describe a perennial tension between two equally important commodities. So, the "solution" doesn't make the problem go away; the "solution" involves caring well for opposite sides of the equation and keeping both in balance. It's a both-and dynamic in which the health of each side depends on managing the health of the other.

Let's consider three universal polarities:

- *Self and Other.* These kinds of ongoing, committed relationships include marriage and parenting at home and all vertical and horizontal relationships at work. These are not problems to be solved but true polarities that must be managed. They require equal degrees of respect for self and respect for the other, honesty with self and honesty with the other, care for self and care for the other. An imbalance in this universal polarity will inevitably damage one side or the other.
- *Being and Doing.* Although the emphasis may shift somewhat from season to season, there is an intrinsic connection between who we are in our essential identity and what we do in our actions. All "doing" flows out of "being," yet "being" must express itself in authentic "doing." Western culture, and the business world in particular, tend to over-emphasize the performance side of this equation and damage the "being" side through neglect. Great leaders manage this polarity by attending to both the humanity of their people as well as providing accountability for their work responsibilities. Again, not a problem to be solved but a polarity to be managed.
- *Leader and Context.* This is the polarity we've been addressing throughout this chapter. Every leader must have followers or an organizational context in which to lead. There are no leaderless organizations! Organizations exist because leaders have distributed power and influence within a structure in order to accomplish a specific mission, hence the interdependent relationship between individual and context.

SYMPTOMS AND CONSEQUENCES

Earlier in the chapter, we talked about the potential imbalances in the Individual-Context relationship and represented those with a small "you" bubble and a big "work" bubble (Figure 1.2) and also the other danger point: a big "you" bubble and a small "work" bubble (1.3). Now it's time to describe the symptoms and consequences of those imbalances, starting with a window into Rob's story:

I must have been around thirty-two years old when I flew to Green Bay for my annual visit to Troy Murphy, my friend and mentor. Troy was one of the few older men in my life who wasn't afraid to push past my confident exterior nor be put off by my bluster. He had firmly decided at some point in our growing relationship that he was "for me," regardless. There was little I could do to change his position, and this commitment has become proven over decades.

This is not only a rare gift for someone as guarded as myself—someone who tends to sabotage relationships for fear that the vulnerable parts would get exposed or taken advantage of, but also rare in a self-centered leadership culture that often uses relational commitment merely as a means to get ahead.

"I'm bored, Troy." After we got through the pleasantries, he had asked how I was really doing, and that was my most honest answer. My life had gotten pretty settled by this point. We'd made a bold move from California to Nashville a few years before, bought our first house, and I was working in the family business. The wild adventures of our twenties had been replaced by the more sober responsibilities of our thirties, and I felt like I was finally having to be a grownup.

Troy's response was compassionate but direct. "I don't think you're bored. I think you're under-challenged." The words took me aback and made me look at my situation from a fresh perspective. Maybe my lack of enthusiasm to get out of bed in the mornings wasn't disappointment or apathy with my life as much as just a lack of opportunity to dig and go deeper.

On the flight home, I began to let my imagination engage that question: What steps could I take that would bring fresh challenge? My first decision was to enroll in a master's degree. I suppose any number of opportunities could have provided that kind of push for me, but diving into new ideas and assignments quickly pushed me out of "bored" into fully engaged. I felt electric as the blood returned to my veins and began to flow again. Most days I was working hard to integrate what I was learning, and some days I wondered if I was going to make it. But I did, and that only further fueled the polarity balance.

It was maybe a year later, however, when things began to shift again. We unexpectedly had our fourth child, and I made a decision to transition out of the family business to start my first company, all at the same time. These decisions piled on and flung me into a season of being severely over-challenged. Life was full on and I was running hard. Too hard. It felt exciting at times but unsustainable. In those two years, I had swung from one side of the polarity pendulum to the other, and I had to make concessions to find a more centered position.

Looking from the viewpoint of our current lives, we can see our history through the lens of these simple diagrams—times when the imbalance between our inner resources and the context of life left us feeling under- or over-challenged and what it took to reclaim that balance. There's nothing wrong with getting to one of those points; most of us will face both sides of that polarity multiple times in our journey. It's what we do at that point that matters. Extended feelings of boredom or stress are signals that the polarity needs to be realigned. Trouble follows when we're not paying attention to the signals.

Perhaps this is a good time to clarify that perfect balance is unattainable. The goal isn't to never swing from side to side; it's to simply be aware of when we do and know when we need to make adjustments. Even the imbalances serve important and necessary purposes when we leverage them for growth. *We have to become good at all the positions and harness the power of all of them.*

When leaders remain under- or over-challenged for any length of time, it invites problems, and the most common problems cluster around the themes of burnout, numb-out, or in more extreme cases, a flame-out. The response of burnout is associated with being over-challenged for an extended period of time and usually manifests as *extreme anxiety, control,* and *stress.* Being under-challenged for an extended period of time can show up as *boredom, apathy,* and *depression.* Individuals at these extremes usually end up having to manage and medicate themselves to survive and cope with the symptoms, often becoming dependent or addicted to such things as over-eating, under-eating, working, sex, substance abuse, over-exercising, video games, shopping, or the plethora of other forms of escape.

Flame-outs can happen in either of these two scenarios: conscious or subconscious actions taken in an attempt to stop the bleeding. Flame-outs are the more self-destructive dynamics we observe, things like self-sabotaging your job, your marriage, or even your own safety.

We are not mental health professionals, so we can't address the types and treatments for these maladies. Our interest is in helping you find ways to pay attention to your polarities as a way of avoiding these kinds of distress and maximizing your long-term leadership health.

As a leader, it's imperative that you understand the organic nature of both poles. Neither people nor organizations are mechanical entities. When leaders begin to treat their people, either individually or corporately, like a machine, bad things happen. In an impersonal, mechanistic environment, the soul begins to starve. When people feel like fodder to drive the industrial engine of commerce, inspiration and loyalty evaporate, and all that remains is the lowest modicum of effort to keep a paycheck coming, while the resume gets dusted off.

We can do better than that. *We must do better than that!* Both individuals and organizations are made for something that inspires and elevates, that creates value and builds connection. We are made for meaning. We have to breathe, both in our individual lives as well as our organizational context.

In our next chapter, we're going to introduce you to the HOS, the four quadrants of being that have the potential to empower our personal and professional lives with meaning, passion, and mission.

REFLECTION QUESTIONS

1. *Draw your Leader-Context polarity on a piece of paper and describe how you are functioning, both at home and work. Is your balance healthy or dysfunctional?*

2. *Name any symptoms you're experiencing that could indicate being over-challenged or under-challenged in your current leadership environment.*

3. *Which core competency needs your immediate attention, and what is your plan for developing this competency?*

4. *What is one action you most need to make right now in order to bring the Human Polarity back into balance?*

2

EMBODYING THE TRUE SELF

Integrating the Four Quadrants

Richard was poised for success. As the newly hired president of a burgeoning medical device company, he was the heir-apparent to take the helm from Bill, the retiring CEO. But when they invited me (Jack) to moderate the conversation, the road was rocky between them.

Listening to them each describe the dynamics in their relationship, I began to pick up on a disconnect in the way they were occupying the HOS, so I invited them into an experiential exercise that walked them through the quadrant realities (which we will explore shortly). What became apparent was that Bill functioned as a highly collaborative leader, while Richard was a strategic thinker who found it difficult to respect the CEO's slower, more relational approach. Richard had a hard time masking his impatience, and the two leaders were not connecting with one another completely. Both were frustrated.

In my exercise, I helped them discern their comfort zones and explained how they could grow their leadership capacity if they could learn to value the other quadrants and cross the thresholds that separated them. Bill was amenable, but Richard just couldn't bring himself to respect a leadership style different than his own. The rejection felt personal and stung Bill deeply.

Meanwhile, Sam, the CFO who had earned Bill's trust over the years by valuing his relational priorities, made his own bid for the company. This served to heighten the tension within the executive leadership team even further, but in the end, Sam's bid was accepted by the Board of Directors. Richard lost the opportunity to acquire the majority shares and lead the company into a new generation of success, all because of a mismanaged HOS. Both the president and the EVP of Business Development were forced out of the company later that year and their business careers subsequently floundered. This case study highlights HOS Principle #2: *Leadership growth requires the integration of Heart, Soul, Mind, and Strength.*

We have witnessed many scenarios like this one in our work with Transformed Leader. Skills and smarts are simply not enough to propel women and men into effective leadership. There has to be more. And the more comes by installing a fully developed, agile HOS, and we're going to unpack the core construct of that system now.

Figure 2.1 shows how four dimensions of reality function as the kernel of the HOS and provide a basis for personal and professional development and change management.[4] Organizational development pioneer Will McWhinney created the conceptual framework represented in this chart, and the opportunity to study personally under his mentorship planted a seed inside me, a seed that would eventually grow into the HOS, a spiritual-psychological development paradigm for mission-driven leaders. I (Jack) will always be indebted to Will's seminal insights as the origin of our work here.

Essentially, these four quadrants represent ways of being in the world as well as the opportunity for integrating all four dimensions into a healthy, empowered whole. Effective leaders are those who are willing and able to learn the language of each quadrant and then find a pathway for harnessing the unique contributions of each quadrant into the various facets of their life and leadership.

The quadrants really are not unlike foreign languages, and learning a new one requires mastering the fundamentals of vocabulary, syntax, and grammar. Each "language" brings its own unique perspective on reality, and the transformational leader is one who can learn each fluently. Every global culture has its own language and meaning system that requires careful interpretation and contextualization. When we don't communicate in the language and culture of those we serve, natural resistance arises to our leadership initiatives.

This, of course, was the exact scenario that led Richard to inadvertently sabotage his path of succession. If he had been willing and able to learn a new language of the Heart and value a different leadership culture with its unique contributions, he would not only have secured his financial future, he would

DIMENSIONS OF HUMAN REALITY

MIND	STRENGTH
Unitary Worldview	Sensory Worldview
POLICIES	ACTIONS
RULES	BEHAVIORS
THEORIES	FACTS
TRUTHS	DATA
CREEDS	OBJECTS
PRINCIPLES	MATERIAL THINGS
DESIGNS	RESOURCES
BELIEF SYSTEMS	EVENTS
STRUCTURES	EXPERIENCES
ASSUMPTIONS	SENSUALITY
WHAT WILL WE DO?	**HOW SHALL WE DO IT?**

SOUL	HEART
Mythical Worldview	Social Worldview
VISION	VALUES
SYMBOLS	FEELINGS
MEANINGS	PREFERENCES
OPPORTUNITIES	WHAT MATTERS
METAPHORS	PURPOSES
STORIES	WANTS
DREAMS	MOTIVATIONS
INVENTIONS	RELATIONSHIPS
INSPIRATIONS	ATTITUDES
CREATIONS	APPRECIATION
WHY SHOULD WE DO IT?	**WHO WILL DO IT?**

Figure 2.1

have begun his journey toward integration—a journey that would have benefited him even more than his stock options.

INTRODUCING THE QUADRANTS

We have taken McWhinney's four worldviews and attached them to our four categories, as you can see in this diagram: Heart, Soul, Mind, and Strength. From the classical philosophers of Plato and Aristotle to the biblical authors to modern psychiatrists such as Freud and Jung, it was common to adopt a trichotomy to explain the different parts of the human experience. Mind, soul, body (Plato); body, soul, and spirit (Saint Paul); id, ego, and superego (Freud)—these were all attempts to explain the numinous qualities of our being.

But it was none less than Jesus himself who expanded on the Old Testament's three-way division (heart, soul, strength) by offering the fourth component (mind) through which to love and comprehend that which makes us human. These are the four essential elements of the HOS. Let's briefly describe each.

Mind. This dimension describes *the strategic center* of our being—that part of us that organizes and structures our inner and outer worlds into intelligent systems. From this space we seek to understand reality and sort it into logical connections that make sense and provide coherence and safety, for ourselves and others. From the Mind, we build and attach ourselves to theories and truths that provide a container to hold our way of being in the world. It answers the core question of *What*.

Strength. This quadrant describes *the sensory center* of our being—that part of us that allows us to absorb the tactile data around us and convert that information into action. From this space we experience and engage the physical world, gathering resources and adopting behaviors for accomplishing goals. This quadrant is anchored in our bodies and as such, is distinct from the other three internal dimensions of self. It answers the core question of *How*.

Heart. This quadrant describes *the emotive center* of our being—that part of us that feels, values, wills, and connects with others. From this inner space we discover who we are, what we want, and who we want to relate to. From this dimension, we build social constructs, find our tribe, and build a life with and for others. It answers the core question of *Who*.

Soul. This is *the meaning center* of our being—the part of us that seeks to make sense of our lives, our stories, and our purpose in the world. From this space we dream, imagine, and create. We cast a vision for our lives, our families, and our business enterprises and then inspire ourselves and others toward that desired future. This quadrant answers the core question of *Why*.

If we overlay the paradigm of quadrants onto the story with Bill and Richard, we get another whole layer of information. In the growing tension between the president and CEO, Richard was a Mind guy, and his failure to understand and value the language of the Heart represented by Bill eventually caused the breakdown in their professional relationship. Both men were one-dimensional in their ability to communicate their quadrant perspectives and resolve issues across quadrants. If either or both of these men had been capable of transcending more than one dimension of reality, the outcome would have been entirely different.

As an upper-quadrant leader (Mind – Strength), Richard couldn't bring himself to respect the values of a lower quadrant leader (Heart – Soul), a common struggle. Achieving results in the top quadrants had far greater value in his perspective than the potential contributions that could have been made from the bottom quadrants. The upper quadrants dominate our entrepreneurial culture and tend to get rewarded for their focus on strategy and action. Rarely is a lower quadrant leader recognized and rewarded for prioritizing and building a healthy culture based on relationships of trust.

In many sectors of our society, short-term results still outweigh the contributions that allow for long-term health. This ship is starting to turn, but it's taking time. Part of our vision in this book is to put our hand on the tiller and encourage a course that brings together the power and genius of all four quadrants, top and bottom.

META-PRAXIS AND INTEGRATION

While we recognize the understandable fixations and limitations in business that isolate the upper-quadrant approach, our goal is not to elevate the lower quadrants above the upper. Instead, our vision is to integrate all four in a change process that is truly transformative. The ability to transcend one particular worldview or cultural context and see the whole in relation to the parts—and how the parts can be utilized for structural and systemic change—is what we call meta-praxis. *Meta-praxis, for our purposes, is the art and science of integrating the four worldviews of the HOS in such a way that the change process empowers a comprehensive way of being and a mature expression of leadership.*

Becoming an integrated leader is a powerful expression of one's *True Self* in contrast to performing out of the *Ideal Self*. For example, achievement-oriented leaders imagine themselves to be successful through the accomplishment of results. Such leaders gain the respect of their peers and the rewards of their profession when they outperform the expectations of their role. If these high-performing leaders have any doubts, fears, or weaknesses, they repress them and maintain the image of being strong, confident, and in control. This is the Ideal Self, and this level of inauthenticity—which we all bear at some level—functions like a virus within the OS, corrupting the files on our internal quadrant work.

There is another threat to the True Self as well. As the Ideal Self attempts to mask what is considered weak or shameful with commodities that appear more valuable within the organization, certain elements of our personalities get intentionally relegated to the shadow. What gets buried in the *Shadow Self* is the fear, doubt, and anxiety that comes from relying upon willpower—an extremely limited resource. The Shadow Self becomes the repository for hiding the emotional parts of Heart and Soul that feel vulnerable. As we exile those unpresentable parts of ourselves and lock them in the basement of our being, the Ideal Self asserts itself with artificial confidence. But this dissonance is unsustainable, and sooner or later, hairline fractures appear on the façade. Managing the "exiles" becomes an exhausting full-time job.

In this psychological drama, pride and shame become powerful forces that the leader struggles to manage by detaching in order to perform. Detaching from the Heart quadrant, in particular, leads to various compulsions, addictive behaviors, and the tendency to manage through domination and control. We explored this briefly in chapter one. Ironically, the greater the investment of personal identity that the high performing leader makes in self-image, the more it undermines true self-esteem.

Authentic and integrated leadership is based on accepting and surrendering to our True Self, embodying the essence of who we are as represented by the Mind, Heart, Soul, or Strength. We must counter-intuitively befriend our Shadow Self and learn to accept the parts of us that feel weak or vulnerable. This is a complex process, and we won't delve into it here, but it's important to understand that the HOS is a powerful force for personal growth for those seeking to live out the full measure of their identity and make their unique contribution in the world. That journey invites us to let go of the Ideal Self with its pretenses, postures, and pressures to embrace a more holistic and authentic posture of being.

Zach began this journey toward his True Self in early 2018. An inner discontent had been working on him for months when he saw an interview in which I (Rob) was talking about my "Tin Man" moment, the story I shared with you in the Introduction. A nameless hunger awoke inside him, and he asked to meet with me for coffee.

Zach was a smart, savvy leader and, like many leaders, had learned the instinctive art of dodging authenticity with transparency. He tested me with a bit of disclosure. Would this be a safe place? Would he be accepted if he let down his performance mask and acknowledged his shortcomings? But disclosure can also be a red herring—turning the conversation away from the more vulnerable and crucial truths of the Heart.

I didn't take the bait but instead invited him to ask the hard questions of himself: *What is it that your heart really wants? What parts of yourself are you afraid of? What did you receive and not receive from your father?* The father angle touched a nerve, and we began to dig underneath the safe, superficial answers. Zach was using a lot of words, but he still seemed detached from his feelings. It was as if he was speaking about someone else.

I asked Zack if he was ready to move from his Mind to his Heart, if he was ready to take a step toward real authenticity. I could see his struggle as he wrestled with the cost of letting go of his denial and actually coming to terms with the deeper truth of his life. His well-honed coping mechanisms started to loosen their grip as he got in touch with the unmet desires of his Heart. Zack was willing to listen to the voices of the young boy, the adolescent boy, and the young man—the voices clamoring for connection and grieving the relationship they never received.

This began Zack's journey toward his True Self, and it has sparked a process of utter transformation. Everything about him is different now. Sure, life is still challenging, but he sees himself more honestly these days, both the good and the bad, and he keeps showing up to tell the truth about all of it. The practice of authenticity has not only reconnected him to himself but also to those around him, especially his boys, who are getting to know their father in ways Zack never knew his own. Zack's movement toward vulnerability has empowered his leadership on every level.

THRESHOLDS OF MATURE LEADERSHIP

The process of becoming a mature leader requires unusual depth and commitment to a developmental process or journey through four levels of leadership. In Figure 2.2 we envision them as a spiral, where the motivated leader moves through the challenges that are presented by each threshold: 1) becoming an Authentic Leader of Individuals, 2) growing as an Integrated Leader of Teams, 3) developing as a Transformational Leader of Organizations, and finally, 4) maturing into a Transcendent Leader of Leaders. Each of these levels of leadership has certain characteristics that need to be developed before we can cross our current threshold to perform as a powerful and effective leader at the next stage of development.

As you read our descriptions of the levels, resist the urge to peg yourself by function: Oh, I lead an organization so that means I'm a Transformational Leader. Not necessarily. These leadership thresholds reflect the inner work of moving around all four quadrants and incorporating their wisdom into your life and leadership. We call this work "taking laps," and it requires the humility of recognizing we can't upgrade our external leadership without upgrading our internal formation. This truth of the polarity will always bind one to the other. Now let's look at the levels themselves.

Level One: Authentic Leader of Individuals

At this initial stage of development, the leader is learning how to be trustworthy, genuine, and integrous as a person. Learning to be authentic is telling the truth about what it feels like to be you in light of your hopes, dreams, and visions. The leadership challenge faced in the first "lap" through the quadrants is labeled as *Character to Inspire* in our diagram. Over time, the prevailing business culture in the western world has shifted from character-based to personality-based, leading to an undue elevation of success and financial results at the expense of great character.

As the aspiring leader makes her first circuit through the quadrants, the opportunity is to develop a meaningful sense of self, to learn to relate in a

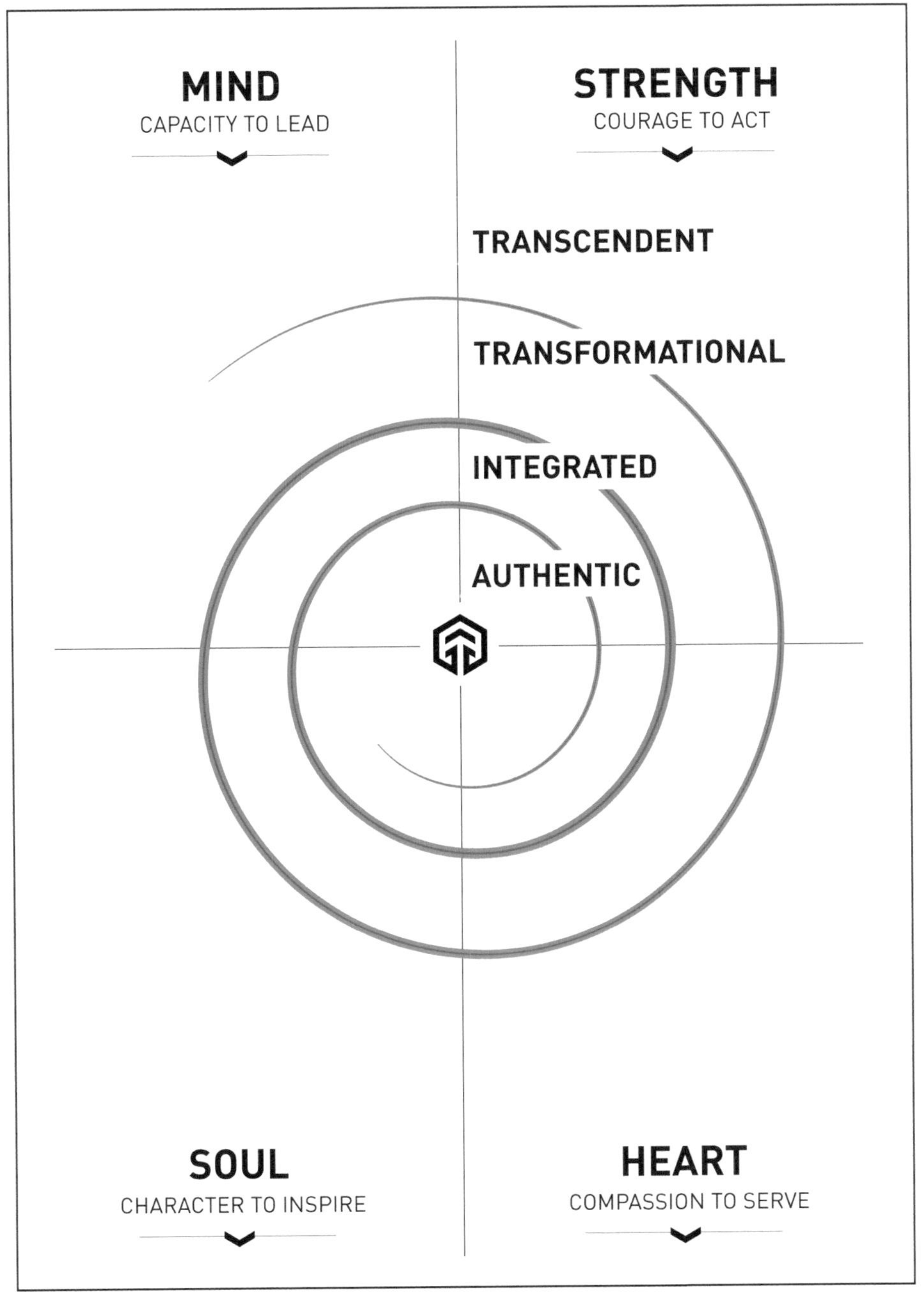
LEADERSHIP THRESHOLDS
MIND
CAPACITY TO LEAD
STRENGTH
COURAGE TO ACT
TRANSCENDENT
TRANSFORMATIONAL
INTEGRATED
AUTHENTIC
SOUL
CHARACTER TO INSPIRE
HEART
COMPASSION TO SERVE

Figure 2.2

healthy way with others, and to demonstrate personal authenticity both at work and at home. There is congruence in what she says and does: what is seen on the outside is slowly becoming consistent with the essential core on the inside. The organizational impact of such authentic leadership flows out of her inspiration as a trustworthy team member who accepts responsibility and is accountable for self-leadership. Organizations need to recruit, develop, and retain Authentic Leaders in order to accomplish their mission.

The leadership pathway for growing in character includes making an investment in leadership coaching and counseling, where one's True Self is identified and supported toward developing as a person and leader. Discovering one's learned and innate talents, strengths, and unique abilities in this phase is essential for the alignment of leadership roles and responsibilities with the organizational mission. This pathway is a difficult discernment process if done in isolation. Having a mentor or coach greatly accelerates the leader's growth as he or she meets the challenges and tests of leadership and can learn to respond in a way that develops character and consistency.

Level Two: Integrated Leader of Teams

The next stage of development as a leader is to become more whole, complete, and integrated in terms of one's Heart and Soul. This is essential if one is to lead a team or engage in group processes because a healthy awareness of self allows for better harnessing of the relational dynamics of a team. If a leader is unaware of her own feelings, it is very difficult to achieve accurate empathy for other people's feelings and perspectives when resolving team tension and conflict. The challenge at this threshold is to integrate the light and dark sides of one's leadership. The Integrated Leader must be awakened in her capacity for the *Compassion to Serve*. Servant-leadership requires compassion for the limitations and complexities of life and the desire to serve through offering your highest and best contributions for human flourishing.

The leadership pathway for becoming an Integrated Leader is doing shadow work. Every leadership challenge will present three choices: *What would the Ideal Self do? What would the Shadow Self do? And what will the True Self finally decide?* The only way that you can develop emotional and social intelligence is to consistently work those three perceptual positions and make the best, most integrated decision possible in your leadership context. Over time, your core motivational values will be clarified and tested in the marketplace of competing priorities. The Integrated Leader will learn to manage ongoing tensions and defensiveness and still be able to resolve conflict and meet the challenges of team leadership. This capacity to resolve complex issues and lead constructive change prepares the way for transformational leadership to emerge.

Level Three: Transformational Leader of an Organization

If leaders become integrated enough to effectively lead themselves and a team, then they will be ready to begin to cross the threshold of organizational leadership. At this threshold of development, the Transformational Leader embraces the weight of responsibility of growing and sustaining a healthy enterprise. This cannot be done through charisma, talent, or willpower alone, but through the development and empowerment of talented people. Transformational Leaders must be continuously renewing and reforming the vision, mission, and strategic direction of the entire organization to keep it in its prime, while continuing to provide the personal mentoring support cultivated at Level Two.

When difficult decisions have to be made, the leader must have the *Courage to Act* in the best interests of both the employees and the enterprise. The Transformational Leader is willing to serve as the catalyst for systemic and structural renewal that fosters individual, team, and organizational health.

Rising to this level of leadership cannot be learned through reading leadership books, participating in workshops, or taking academic courses at business schools. It is earned by courageously crossing the thresholds of the first two stages of leader development—becoming an Authentic Leader of self and others and an Integrated Leader of groups. At that point, and not before, a seasoned commitment from the leader allows her to cross the next threshold to lead an enterprise, where she is constantly tested in the crucible of executive decision-making. The weight of these decisions can be heavy and relentless, but they forge the internal strength to be a high-capacity leader.

The experiential process by which a high-capacity leader can be prepared and fully developed as a Transformational Leader is this: *Transformational Leadership is developed and embodied through engaging each leadership challenge with integrity right at the edge of one's growth.*

Level Four: Transcendent Leader of Leaders

Transcendent leadership is generative, heroic, redemptive, and also very rare. Don't think that simply because you have other leaders as direct reports, that you have crossed this final threshold. The integrative and transformative work that Transcendent Leaders have done in their own souls causes their influence to transcend the limitations of job descriptions and organizational boundaries.

A historical example is found in the life and leadership of Nelson Mandela who spent twenty-seven years in prison, yet attained worldwide influence for the cause of racial parity. Eventually, his transcendence led him to become the first black and democratically elected president of South Africa. In his autobiography, *Long Walk to Freedom*, it was his own personal and spiritual growth in the confines of prison that led to the triumph of his leadership.[5] Paradoxically, the prison walls at Robben Island could not limit his growing influence because of who he was as a man and a leader. He was able to transcend the institutional racism of apartheid to transform the political structure of his nation, and his personal transformation painfully forged through struggle, suffering, persecution, and steadfast hope fueled his *Capacity to Lead* a nation through moral and racial reconciliation.

Not everyone is going to have the international impact of a Nelson Mandela; however, there are certain characteristics that Transcendent Leaders have in common: They have embodied their essence in order to mentor other authentic, integrated, and transformational leaders on their journey. They serve as wise sages to those who want to become leaders of destiny and contribute to human flourishing. They often draw people into powerful leadership communities that multiply the influence and impact of other missional leaders. Transcendent Leaders seize historic challenges and fulfill significant callings for reconciliation and redemption, yet their greatest legacy is mentoring and multiplying other Transformational Leaders to lead mission-driven organizations of significance.

It's worth noting that becoming a Transcendent Leader is not something that a person can choose or make of oneself. Like Mandela, it requires a long journey of personal transformation and the convergence of that experience with the challenge of a unique historical, social, or cultural context. Ultimately, *it is a spiritual quest* that you can prepare for but cannot initiate. It takes unusual depth and commitment for a leader to embrace a transcendent cause that is greater than oneself or even the missional enterprise or organization that one serves. Becoming wise, gracious, and mature enough to be a Transcendent Leader of leaders is a difficult but incredibly meaningful threshold to cross. Will you prepare yourself for such a crossing?

HOLDING THE EDGE OF YOUR GROWTH

Facing a leadership challenge at the edge of one's growth is a place of vulnerability, a feeling most of us don't immediately embrace. That discomfort often leads us to make snap decisions to gain a false sense of being in control, pretending to have a solution when there isn't one. But that's simply posing with the Ideal Self. It takes humility and integrity to hold the Edge of Your Growth without flinching.

Staying right at the edge of one's growth is where a leader can do his or her shadow work, trusting that a deeper wisdom will be revealed to resolve complex systemic issues. It takes courage to explore the light and dark side of one's leadership that might be contributing to the organizational impasse. Systemic problems defy linear solutions, and it requires unusual insight on the part of the leader to know how to move ahead. This insight might come from reflection, wise counsel, deep work, or even sustained contemplative prayer. Often, something needs to shift in the Heart and Soul of the leader before constructive change can occur.

It's a very human tendency to project the need for change onto the leadership team or organization rather than holding the tension until there is a shift in our own mindset, core values, or leadership identity. This is the hard work of personal transformation that a leader cannot avoid or escape but must be worked through in order to lead an organization at the highest levels.

When we first meet with leaders who are interested in growth, we begin by testing their receptivity to taking laps through the quadrants. We want to discern their willingness to cross over from the common leadership approach that is overly reliant on thinking smarter and working harder. We invite them to start the journey to authenticity by taking their first lap around all four quadrants of their being. Authenticity is not something you simply achieve; it's an intangible leadership trait that becomes embodied over months and years of practicing, experiencing, and testing.

These first laps around the quadrants are often terrifying for leaders, yet exhilarating. As they begin to recover and access more of who they are, particularly in the Heart and Soul quadrants, they begin to redefine who they are and how they operate. These brave souls are not, however, always met with smiles and excitement as they begin to become more authentic; there is often a season of wrestling that must be done in each stage of growth. Wrestling to not only say yes to the process, but to keep saying yes and to trust that who they are becoming is valuable, necessary, and important despite resistance from others who are entrenched in a one- or two-dimensional way of being.

At every turn of each lap at every stage of this lifelong journey, there are signposts that lead to the treasure: Character to Inspire, Compassion to Serve, Courage to Act, and Capacity to Lead. Character, compassion, courage, and capacity—these are the treasures. They cannot be bought, stolen, or fabricated, but they can be deepened over time as a leader learns how to incarnate them through their laps around the quadrants on the road from authentic to transcendent leadership.

GOING BENEATH THE LINE

Not long ago, I (Rob) was standing in the presidential conference room in the headquarters of a significantly large company, surrounded by dozens of their top executives—plus others on video screens from international locations. We had been invited by another consulting firm to partner with them in helping the organization explore possible reasons why employee turnover was high. Strategic planning and sound execution had led them to expansion and profit, but their culture was struggling. From our surveys, we uncovered a trend that suggested many of their people felt as if they were commodities, which perpetuated the lack of commitment we were noticing within the organization. We were glad to have been invited into their struggle, believing our collaborative strengths and contributions could work together to recover more Heart and Soul within the organization.

You can imagine the caliber of these men and women; most of them oversaw divisions larger than many entire corporations. It would be easy to feel intimidated. This particular session was focused on exactly what we've been describing in this chapter: crossing thresholds of leadership growth, specifically working through resistance, tension, and conflict right at the edge of growth. These moments between what is and what is becoming can be scary, messy, and disorienting.

To illustrate the nature of thresholds, I began with a personal story. My wife and I got married relatively young and proceeded to have two unplanned children early on. We loved them both dearly and welcomed them enthusiastically, but we also had to acknowledge some genuine loss. We were young, in love, and full of adventure; we had imagined chasing our dreams around the world with utter abandon. And while we wouldn't trade our precious children for anything, I was wrestling with the disappointment of a lost vision.

I remember standing in our small apartment on the hills of San Clemente when our second child Ella Jane was about four months old, and the struggle reached its apex. I knew I had to let go of what was lost in order to fully embrace what I had been given, but I had been dragging my feet. Finally, the dam broke and with tears, I threw my hands up in the air in defeat, fell to my knees, and shouted to God and the world, "Okay, okay! I will be a dad. I will be a dad!" I lay face down on the floor in surrender with broken sobs.

After some time, the grief turned to acceptance, and I slowly stood—the emotional weight rolled off my shoulders—and walked out of the room. I had been a father for several years, but it wasn't until that moment that I became a dad. That moment marked the crossing of a threshold in my life, and I have never turned back. Some have called this a phoenix process; all I know is that I had been stuck in my journey until I was able to cross over into a new season of life and leadership. Most leaders face a tense hesitation to let go of the past, to consciously decide to accept and embrace the next level of growth and development standing in front of them.

Sharing this story of my own crossing, one guy in the requisite dark suit interrupted my illustration with a trace of aggression. "Don't you think you're being a little dramatic with all this imagery about death and resurrection?" As his challenge hung in the air, my inner flow came to a screeching halt.

Our typical instinct in a moment of confrontation is fight, flight, or freeze, and my personal bent is usually to fight, rising up to meet the energy of the person challenging me. But in that micro-second of pause, I reached for another, truer alternative by making a quick circuit of my quadrants: In my Soul, I affirmed the meaning of my message and relevance of my story as a personal metaphor; in my Heart, I acknowledged my feelings, including the fear of possibly losing credibility among these leaders; at the Strength quadrant, I recognized my shadow motivations to crush this guy and beat him at his own game; but in my Mind, I saw how my illustration had structurally and emotionally disrupted this executive's value system. In his world of think-smarter and work-harder, there was no room for the vulnerability and unpredictability of Heart and Soul. Behind his challenge, he appeared deeply uncomfortable with going beneath the line into the lower quadrants.

My furious internal processing complete, I answered him evenly, "You would say that because you're an American, just like me. We tend to be uncomfortable with feelings and mystery." I had met his challenge, but I wasn't being reactive, but rather genuinely responsive. As the room digested our exchange, one of the European leaders spoke through his video screen to support me. "I agree with Rob. I don't think he's being dramatic enough."

At that point, the CEO chuckled loudly beside me, breaking the tension and affirming that the entire exchange had only proven my point. We went on to use that moment as a perfect example of the challenges we face as we attempt to cross thresholds and our collective discomfort in going beneath the line to become more resourced and holistic in our leadership. As Americans, we have become so focused on strategy and execution that to sprinkle any mystery, imagery, or metaphor feels overly dramatic and unnecessary. Counterproductive even. Meanwhile, a more global perspective on the same story says that it's not dramatic enough.

There are some well-managed companies (not all) who struggle to prioritize their cuture by investing in the growth and development of their people. It's an understandable challenge when stock prices and company valuations become the critical metrics that matter most for shareholders, owners, and decision makers. This type of pressured business environment can create an organizational culture that only values bottom-line results. As Robert Quinn observes, "Most of us build our identity around our knowledge and competence in employing certain known techniques and abilities. Making a deep change involves abandoning both and 'walking into the land of uncertainty.' This is usually a terrifying choice, often involving a 'dark night of the soul.' It is therefore natural for each of us to deny that there is any need for a deep change."[6]

Integrative approaches desire to harness the power of the upper quadrants but also builds upon the solid foundation of the lower quadrants. Mind and Strength serve us well, but aligned with Heart and Soul, the organization can function at the full measure of its potential and capacity to live, love, and lead.

REFLECTION QUESTIONS

1. *How would you engage one of your current leadership challenges from the positions of your Ideal Self, your Shadow Self, and finally, your True Self?*

2. *Which of the four quadrants—Heart, Soul, Mind, or Strength—is most natural or comfortable for you, and why?*

3. *Which leadership threshold are you struggling to cross over at this time? What feels difficult, messy, or intimidating on the edge of that potential growth?*

4. *Who would be a good sage, mentor, or coach that would help you navigate your current leadership challenge? How would you go about choosing that kind of guide or mentor?*

3

FINDING YOUR FLOW

Engaging Your Unique Design and Contributions

Having climbed the ladder on Wall Street with elegance and precision, Sarah had recently taken a position in Tennessee, where the slower pace of life had left her disoriented, wanting to learn how to manage the effects of a career and location change. That quest had brought Sarah to our office, and we were trying to discern what was most important to her.

Typically, when engaging a new client, we like to describe the basic quadrants of the HOS and invite him or her to experience it with us firsthand. It creates a more powerful, visceral introduction to our work than merely teaching concepts.

Sarah was game. "Where do we start?"

Having shared with her the essential substance of Heart, Soul, Mind, and Strength, we asked her, "Which of the four quadrants do you gravitate toward first?"

She didn't hesitate. "Mind! I was born for strategy, structure, and frameworks."

We asked her a follow-up. "If you start in the Mind, which quadrant do you generally go to next? Which direction does your energy flow?"

Again, her reply was immediate. "Strength. I go from Mind to Strength."

Her answers didn't surprise us. The instinctive, confident identification with the upper quadrants is common among marketplace leaders for reasons we have already discussed. Clearly, Sarah had made a place for herself and advanced in her career by mastering these very attributes of cogent thinking and effective action. She had carved out her niche as a mover and shaker in the fiercely competitive environment of Wall Street, so this was comfortable territory for her.

Knowing that identification within the quadrants can come from two places — either adaptation to the prevailing values of the current culture or a truer, deeper understanding of personal essence (what we call the True Self) — we gently pressed on Sarah's conclusions by asking curiously, "Have you always been this way?"

Momentarily disrupted, she wavered. We could sense that she was doing a rewind of her life in seconds, scanning for clues to answer truthfully, and she found something.

Her lips began to quiver, her body began to slump, and a lone tear rolled down her cheek. "I was a Heart person once." Trying to manage her rising emotion, she said it again. "I was a Heart person. But there's no place for a heart on Wall Street, so what does it matter anyway?"

We sat quietly in the sacred presence of that revelation before asking her the next question. "What would it cost you to release your determined grip on that independence, the power you have carved out to succeed in high finance, and start to make room for your heart to beat again?"

"Too much. It would cost me too much." We loved her honest reply.

Even though Sarah wasn't yet ready to cross that threshold in her journey, she learned something priceless that day: that she had sacrificed something essential to her being in her career track but had also learned how to live out of another quadrant in order to survive, and by some measures, thrive. She had gained something—and lost something else. But that something else wasn't gone forever; she just had to decide if and when to re-engage with that vital part of herself to become more integrated. Sarah's story leads us to HOS Principle #3: *Leadership growth is fueled by harnessing your unique design and flow.*

QUADRANT FLOW

The vital parts of ourselves can be elusive, but it lies deep within the human capacity to find meaning and significance in our lives. No one has to teach us this—it's instinctive. We long to unearth the purpose of our existence. With more than thirty years of teaching and writing, Os Guinness says that the most consistent question he gets asked is, "How do I find and fulfill the central purpose of my life?"[7]

In our work with leaders, we see it everywhere: People wrestle with a sense of self-stewardship throughout their journey, seeking to discover, uncover, and recover their truest selves so they can live out of that authentic place at home and work. Frederick Buechner, an American novelist, poet, and theologian said, "The place God calls you to is the place where your deep gladness and the world's deep hunger meet."[8] Do you know where that place is for you? As leaders, we must find it—and lead from it.

Psychologists generally agree that in the list of basic needs, *meaning* and *belonging* are of the utmost importance for a human being. As students of the HOS, we agree. We want to know that our contribution to life is meaningful and that we belong to a tribe. With place and people, we feel safe. People are desperate for a clear path that can help them discover more meaning and purpose. And honestly, that's why we've written this book—to equip leaders to live a truly authentic life.

In the last chapter, we outlined the kernel of the HOS by describing the four quadrants (as seen in Figure 3.1). We went on to describe the developmental journey of leadership across four key thresholds. Now we turn our attention more directly to our quadrants of origin and how we flow through them.

Figure 3.1

YOUR STARTING BLOCK

As we have mentioned previously, Jesus himself identified the following as the greatest commandment: "Love the Lord your God with all your heart and with all your soul and with all your mind and with all your strength."[9] Regardless of your spiritual beliefs, these dimensions of being have been used since ancient times to describe unique parts of ourselves, parts that have the capacity to love and function in different ways. In this sense, the HOS is not innovative or original to us; we are simply tapping into a wealth of knowledge that has not been widely understood or utilized.

We began to flesh out those quadrant descriptions in the last chapter in order to recognize the four dimensions of being that are available for us to resource our lives. In this chapter, we want to recognize that *each of us has a quadrant of origin*: a "home base" that—through a combination of nature and nurture—feels most natural, comfortable, and intuitive for each of us. Not unlike the many personality systems in use today, these four quadrants offer a fresh way of understanding how you show up in the world. These archetypes offer leaders and teams incredible perspectives toward understanding how we love, live, work, contribute, and lead, both personally and professionally. Let's take a look.

As you read through these four brief descriptions, be attentive for the characteristics that feel most authentic to your natural, primary, or dominant way of being—the stance or approach that most reflects your instinctive way of relating to yourself and others. Think about how others have described you, and try to separate the person you think you should be from the person that you already are. Rest assured, none of the four is superior or inferior. We have some of all the quadrants in us, and we have an amazing opportunity to cultivate our further growth in all four of them as well. But one quadrant is often your starting block. In order to develop and integrate, we have to discern where we begin.

Figure 3.2

THE HEART-STARTER

These people enter into projects, relationships, conversations, and the world at large from the position of the Heart. They are feelers, connectors, collaborators, and lovers. Their social worldview motivates them to answer the question, *Who* is with me? Who do I need for this project? Who will this help?

At their best, Heart-Starters lean into their lives in order to connect with people, feelings, wants, and desires. They seek to commune and share their lives with others out of a primal need for belonging. If you have a vision or a project that needs to be done, it's your Soul that offers the inspiration. But your Heart brings the passionate call for others to gather, join, and collaborate. The superpower for Heart-Starters is their *Capacity for Connection* as the fundamental point for action.

At their worst, Heart-Starters may become overly attached to their feelings, seek to please others at the expense of their own mission, or become mired in introspection and inactivity.

Here's how one such leader describes his experience of being in the world as this archetype:

I can't imagine a world without "my people" alongside. I have gone places, done things, and made decisions . . . all because of who invited me. I gravitate toward what feels good and right. In the business world, I rely on this sixth sense constantly: Do I feel a connection with this client? How can I improve the connection with this team? Do I feel valued, seen, appreciated? I rely on my gut to inform and guide my actions—and this can sometimes get me into trouble if I ignore logic or move forward impulsively with unprocessed emotions. But most of the time, this intuition serves me well.

A few months ago, I walked into a meeting with the executive leader of a partner company knowing there was "a disturbance in the force." There would surely be issues to resolve, but I had a single objective: to sense whether they were with me and for me . . . or not.

If they were with me, I would do anything to improve service, drive business, and strengthen our collaboration, but if they weren't, I would have to consider making the costly decision to step away from the partnership. I cannot partner in business with others who don't respect or value my contributions. When I am asked to prove, perform, or justify my value, that is a red flag of an untrustworthy relationship. Fortunately, they affirmed our teamwork, and we were able to find new ways to serve our clients better together. The personal connection is everything for me; when I feel that, I will move heaven and earth to make the partnership work.

Figure 3.3

THE SOUL-STARTER

These people enter into projects, relationships, conversations, and the world at large from the position of the Soul. They are contemplatives, sages, visionaries, and innovators. Imagine Gandalf, from *The Lord of the Rings*. Their mystical worldview motivates them to answer the question, *Why* are we doing this? Why is this important? Why are we going in this direction?

At their best, Soul-Starters are all about vision and deeper meaning, seeking to captivate and inspire others with stories, inventions, symbols, and metaphors. Their capacity to view an unseen reality allows them a grand perspective, which they offer to others as wise counsel. The superpower for this archetype is their *Capacity for Meaning* as a context for everything else.

At their worst, Soul-Starters may isolate themselves in the world of ideas, withdraw when they feel invalidated or misunderstood, or seek safety in exploration without choosing to act.

Here are some perspectives from Natalie, a Soul-based leader and professional bread baker:

Even as a young child, I was called an old soul, a deep well, a person of wisdom. I can't help but look for the depth of perspective behind practicalities. When I show up for a project, I have to connect to the deeper meaning behind it. Activity for activity's sake doesn't work for me. I'm constantly reaching for the inter-connectedness of tasks to the body and to nature. Making bread offers me expression and solidarity with many parts and pieces of this world. Flour, salt, and water are just three ingredients, but they carry a mystical alchemy that mirrors the world at large.

Mysterious is how some experience me, which leads some to lean in with curiosity and others to withdraw in intimidation. And I'm okay with that; tension is comfortable for me. My first instinct is to connect with ideas and symbols more than people, but at the same time, I need people. I'm learning how to move beyond being misunderstood in order to bring my way of seeing the world to the relationships in my life.

Figure 3.4

THE MIND-STARTER

These people enter into projects, relationships, conversations, and the world at large from the position of thought and the Mind. They are the intellectuals, thinkers, designers, and strategists. Their structural worldview motivates them to answer the question, *What* are we doing about this problem? What steps need to happen? What do we need to know?

At their best, they bring things like plans, policies, principles, and beliefs to the forefront of their approach and considerations. Their ability to perceive patterns and relationships allows them to place the pieces and parts together in systems that can deliver the desired results. The superpower for Mind-Starters is their *Capacity for Understanding* the big picture.

At their worst, Mind-Starters may become more attached to the flawless execution of their systems and strategies than to those being served by them, may dismiss perspectives that cannot be logically proved, or may become controlling in their advocacy for process improvements and consistency.

Read how property developer Richard Glass describes his experience of leading from this quadrant:

I like working in property because the slower pace of transactions gives me time to resolve problems and create strategies. I like to figure out the details and mitigate the risk. I see many wheels and cogs in my imagination—all the moving parts to a problem or opportunity. Often, I have to find the missing pieces to make the whole system work. Sometimes I have to risk starting with an incomplete system in faith that the missing pieces will emerge as we go.

The hard part for me is losing track of the people behind the pieces. It's easy for me to assume that everyone is on board when I haven't done the work to generate buy-in, or don't know how to motivate them to buy in. I tend to believe that my ideas are so strong that everyone will naturally fall in line and commit. Another challenge I face is working the details so hard and long that by the time I'm ready to start, I've lost momentum. But I'm learning from my mistakes, and I've begun to find leadership styles and approaches that really amplify my capacity as a Mind-Starter.

Figure 3.5

THE STRENGTH-STARTER

These people enter into projects, relationships, conversations, and the world at large from a bias toward and capacity for physical action. Their greatest energy arises when the meeting ends and it's time to get to work. They are the warriors, the doers, the managers, and drivers who harness the material world to achieve results. Their sensory worldview motivates them to answer the question, *How* will we get it done?

At their best, Strength-Starters bring a catalytic force that transforms intangible ideas into tangible products and activities. They are fast, resourceful, efficient, and direct; they instinctively assess challenges, rally resources, and lead the charge. The superpower for Strength-Starters is their *Capacity for Service* to something greater than themselves.

At their worst, they may disconnect from relationships, meaning, and emotion to become harsh taskmasters. Their sense of urgency may lead them to act prematurely and without a well-formed plan, the consequences of which are then felt tangibly throughout the whole organization or family unit.

I (Rob) will never forget an experience I had several years ago. Our talent agency had brokered a complex deal between a rock band and one of our event clients, but the relationships within the band were falling apart. Two of the lead singers were so at odds with each other that they refused to go on stage together, and the entire deal was in jeopardy.

As a Heart-Starter, I was working all the relational angles, trying hard to be diplomatic and delicate to inspire the various parties to mend fences. There seemed to be no easy outcome that was going to satisfy everyone, but I was committed to strategically and politically facilitate as best I could. Yet I was stymied.

Brian was one of my team members, a Strength-Starter who simply sees and engages the world differently than me. One morning, about five weeks into this little nightmare, I was briefing Brian on the latest frustrations. About three hours later he texted me saying that it had been handled.

"What has been handled?" I replied. I didn't know what he could possibly be talking about.

"The problem you had with those singers. It's fixed. I sorted it out."

I was dumbfounded.

Tapping into his get-it-done energy, Brian had simply rolled up his sleeves and marched into battle. He had called both singers and other key staff and essentially told them to wake up, shut up, show up, and deliver. And they agreed. It was an amazing display of strength, and it got the job done. Brian's take-no-prisoners approach could have backfired; sometimes force is met with resistance. But in this case, it complemented my leadership style perfectly. This is why we need all four quadrant types on the team.

BUILDING THE TEAM

From these simple explanations of the four archetypes and the stories represented for each you can begin to see, not just your own type and how that shapes the unique value you bring to the team, but the value of each of the four types. As much as we have the capacity to grow our types and even cultivate our agility among the other types, we will always carry the particular superpower of our starting position. This means we will always need

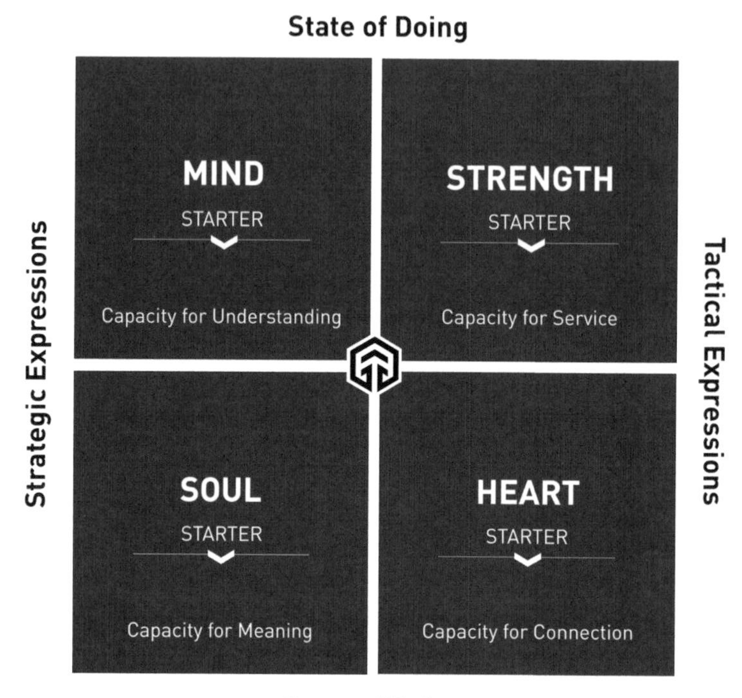

Figure 3.6

the other superpowers of the other types in order to gain a comprehensive leadership matrix. If even one of the archetypes is missing, your team will be handicapped. Let's discuss the reason for this.

As you can see from Figure 3.6, the four quadrants run along two axes. The vertical axis highlights the different emphases on the state of *doing* (top quadrants) and the state of *being* (bottom quadrants), and while you may not have thought in these terms before, both are essential. The priority of *doing* is championed by Mind-Starters and Strength-Starters; these types are energized by and gifted for the accomplishment of tasks. And tasks are important. We've been set into this world in order to live out our purpose, and without that purpose being set in motion, our lives and businesses lose significance. As we've mentioned before, the *doing* side of the equation is what gets the lion's share of attention, resources, and acclaim in our current culture. But there is more. Much more!

The priority of *being* is championed by Soul-Starters and Heart-Starters, and this dimension is usually under-appreciated and under-valued in our culture. *Being* is what fuels *doing*, and without equal attention to the *being* dimension, our tasks lack meaning. They lack context. At the core, they lack identity because purposeful vocation flows out of identity. That is the unique contribution of the Soul-Starter. From the Heart dimension comes the core value of people and relationship, and in our experience in consulting with enterprises, both small and large, we observe that most business failures happen here. Most often it's not failures in product design, marketing, or financial management that bring companies to the ground; it's conflict and burnout and miscommunication that cripple commerce and create lost opportunities.

And there's another axis: *strategic and tactical*. The quadrants on the left side bring a strong capacity to the team for noticing and articulating the visionary and structural parts of the enterprise. The quadrants on the right side bring a capacity to activate the tangible, observable parts of the team—the people and their activity.

These strategic and tactical dimensions can be seen in the simple maxim, *Ready – Aim – Fire. Aiming* is the gift of the strategic—the Soul-Starter and the Mind-Starter—while *Firing* is the gift of the tactical—the Heart-Starter and the Strength-Starter. Sometimes leaders and companies are described by changing the order: *Ready – Fire – Aim*. This bias for action betrays a priority for physical movement that may lack meaning and strategy. It's also possible, though less common, for companies to get preoccupied with the conceptual intangibles at the expense of physical action.

The market has a way of weeding out enterprises that lack a healthy balance on the axis of strategic and tactical. It's the imbalance on *doing* at the expense of *being* that the market will actually reward, even though the cost is high to the Heart and Soul of the enterprise. In this scenario, companies become machines rather than organisms, with high casualties in human resources and altruism. And those losses show up eventually on the bottom line.

The good news is that the HOS offers leaders and organizations the framework and tools for creating a healthy enterprise that is both profitable and meaningful, and when both of those forces come into sync, the benefits are exponential. To tap these opportunities, we have to understand where we start on the quadrants and where we move next.

All archetypes will find a tremendous amount of energy identifying with those who share their type. This feeds the general need we have as humans to find resonance by being known, seen, and understood by those who know what it's like to be you. There is an added nuance, however, for these primary starting positions: understanding where they flow. We begin in one quadrant, and then we naturally flow, gravitate, or move to the secondary quadrant—our next most comfortable habitat—on our way through all four of them.

The entire sequence we take through the four quadrants is illuminating, particularly the starting and ending ones. We start where our perspectives, values, and gifts most instinctively take us. Once we tap those resources, we go to the next most familiar resource: quadrant two.

HEART-STARTERS ON THE MOVE

When the archetype rooted in the Heart quadrant makes a move, this leader has three choices: Heart to Strength, Heart to Mind, or Heart to Soul. Let's unpack them.

1. Heart to Strength: "Feels good. Let's go."

This movement is what I (Rob) resonate with the most as my flow. I approach life, circumstances, projects, and challenges by starting with feelings, motivations, wants, and the gathering of people. From there I cross up above the line into the Strength quadrant and become a person of action. I feel it, then I do it. It's that simple for me in my particular flow through the HOS.

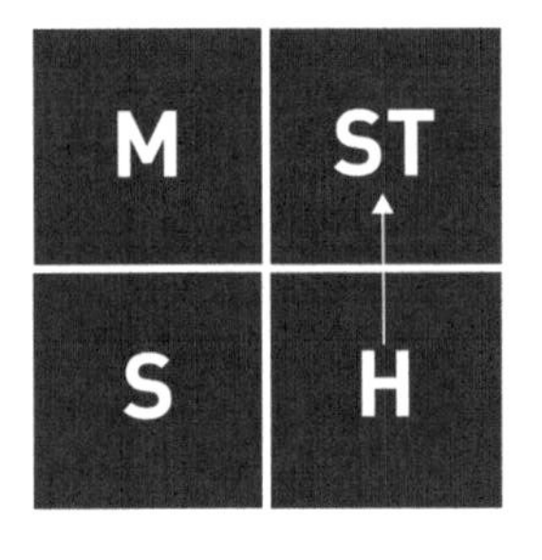

Those who are starting in the Heart align with their superpower, which is capacity for relationship and connection. What they do is first motivated by who they are doing it with. My family and friends know that once I get invested in an idea and have trusted colleagues who are eager to join, something tangible will happen very shortly thereafter. For Heart-to-Strength leaders, the Mind slows them down, and the Soul can often feel too intangible for action. This means we sometimes gather and act before we know why and how. Learning comes through mistakes, exhausted relationships, or abandoned missions.

2. Heart to Mind: "Feels good. Let's understand more."

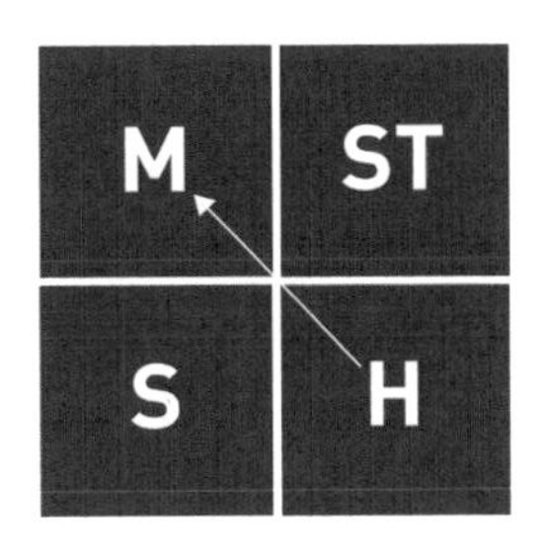

Leaders who go Heart to Mind also move above the line, but it's nuanced in that their relational, internal energy shifts toward information, principles, and strategies rather than going immediately to action. They have assembled their people; now they're looking for a structure to contain, guide, and deepen the connection that is forming among the group.

These are the people whose OS prioritizes values and seeks collaboration with others. They care, and then they consider. The way they evaluate strategies is not solitary; it's by engaging others. Some may do this work alone in the Mind, but their intent is always to bring it back to the team, where they will process openly and revise. Where Heart to Strength connects relationship with action, Heart to Mind unites relationship and strategy. One is not necessarily better than the other; they're simply different, and understanding those differences allow you to align your native talents with the specific needs of your job. It also invites you to build your team with those who have superpowers that are different than your own.

3. Heart to Soul: "Feels good. But why?"

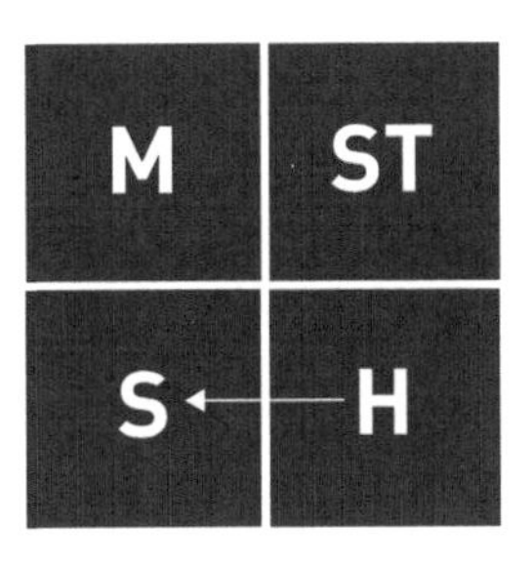

Heart-Starters who move to Soul remain below the line for their two leading quadrants. They represent a somewhat mysterious leadership quality. At best, this archetype (along with the Soul-Starter who moves to Heart) can bring feeling and meaning together through inspirational imagery, metaphor, and story. We would call this type a "heart-felt visionary." In the current leadership culture, this combination struggles to be understood for reasons we've already explained, yet the unique contribution of this type of combination is strong in the HOS. It's worth noting that, because western culture values vision, some leaders aspire or attempt to be visionary, yet the result may lack the essential energy and larger dimensions of the Soul.

Because the Heart-to-Soul leader stays below the line, the being trait of this combination is explosive. Identity, values, purpose, connection—all these commodities are multiplied exponentially, while the *doing* attributes come a little slower. When paired with other doers, this leadership style is particularly effective at creating legacy and multi-generational enterprises. Without doers to carry their inspiration into battle, these leaders may remain stuck, creating possibilities that don't get actualized. The power of imagination allows a Heart to Soul leader to see beyond the black-and-white construct typical in above-the-line leadership to reveal a larger color palette. This ability can stall action in pursuit of an unattainable ideal, or it can identify essential values that are mission-critical.

SOUL-STARTERS ON THE MOVE

Those who are starting in the Soul carry their particular capacity for wisdom, meaning, and perspective forward into the next quadrant. Let's look at these combinations.

1. Soul to Mind: "This is meaningful. Let's design it."

Steve Jobs was the innovator extraordinaire of our generation who embodied the Soul-Starter in the marketplace. Steve would start in Soul but go to Mind, where his visions, designs, and innovations would begin to be shaped by the systems and processes needed to breathe life into them and position them for production. If the structures didn't exist to carry the vision forward, he would invent them. Only after Soul went to Mind did his innovations move to Strength, where Jobs was known to be ruthless in execution. He never set out to create a community per se, but he was able to tell a compelling story—and community gravitates naturally around a great story. Apple's marketing picked up on the Why before the How and began actively building a brand community based on a creative lifestyle.

I (Jack) most resonate with this flow. From the place of creative imagination, I envision ideals and then move to the strategic realm to place those ideals within systems and structures that can be communicated with clarity. Since both of my quadrants reside on the strategic side of the matrix, I carry a strong need to push my creations into the tactical realm, and often need assistance from the Strength quadrant to make that happen. Because of the market's emphasis on execution, there is a danger of Heart being the missing ingredient that is needed to make products or services truly great. So, on the basis of my personal flow within the HOS, I take proactive steps to cultivate the creative-development dimension of my leadership, but I need people who have talents in the Heart and Strength quadrants to drive visionary ideas to production.

2. Soul to Strength: "This is meaningful. Let's build it."

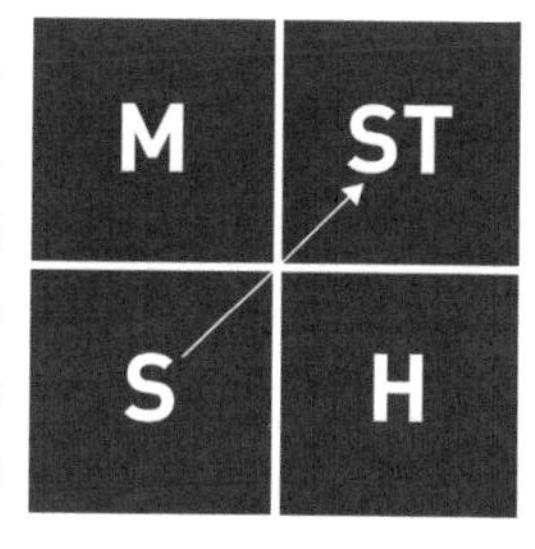

Vision, dreams, and stories are the starting points for the Soul to Strength leader. Once this flow gets inspired, it moves straight to action to make it happen. From *meaning*, this combination moves, sometimes impulsively, to "launch the rocket," sometimes building it while it flies through the air. This leader believes that because this vision matters, it has to work. All we have to do now is just step up and execute on it.

You can see from this description how Soul to Strength crosses the horizontal axis to move from being to doing and also crosses the vertical line from strategic to tactical. Therefore, this particular flow taps all four components at some level. Where the vision can encounter resistance is in bypassing the relational resource of Heart or the strategic resources of Mind. And that's the truth of every flow: it taps one set of vital qualities and misses another. But once we understand the capacities we bring to the table—both from our quadrant of origin and the next quadrant in our flow—we can pair ourselves to the teams and tasks that need us most.

3. Soul to Heart: "This is meaningful. Join me."

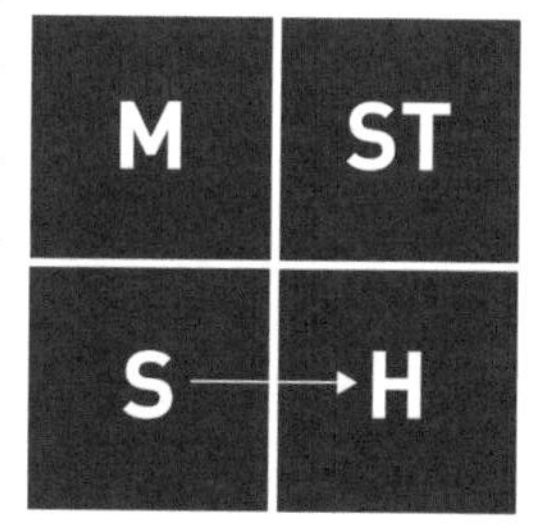

The final path possibility for the Soul-Starter is to move to Heart. This leader can be a "mystical moodmaker," shaping the currents within a room through presence alone. Because of this leader's magnetic pull on others, this quality can scare those who find comfort in the physicality of the upper quadrants. Much like their counterpart Heart to Soul, this leader is easily misunderstood or marginalized within the organization, particularly in companies that demand clear, concise deliverables.

Operating in both quadrants below the line emphasizes the unique (and often disregarded) qualities of being. Along with this asset, Soul to Heart runs the risk of fostering visionary ideas and relationships without moving the project to strategy and action. The marketplace, however, functions as a refining force as it tests visionary ideas and translates them into value propositions where measurables and profits rule.

MIND-STARTERS ON THE MOVE

Leaders who start in the Mind carry a high capacity for understanding. They naturally look for principles and patterns, wanting to know where ideas and processes fit into the larger system. From this stance, they move to one of the other quadrants next. Let's take a look.

1. Mind to Strength: "Makes sense. Let's go."

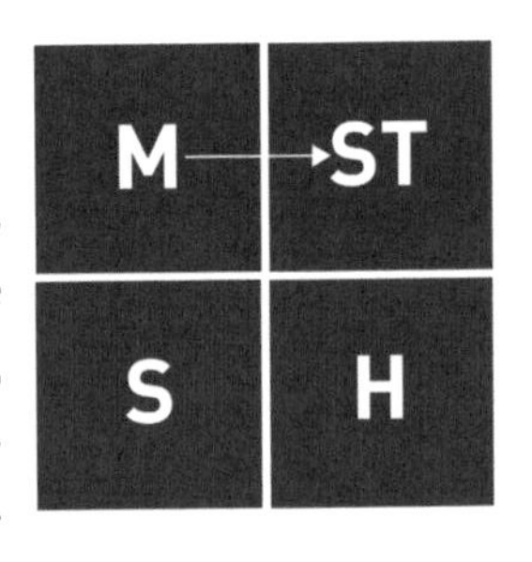

This flow is the polar opposite of the last one because in this scenario both quadrants remain above the line. The strength of *doing* gets doubled, and the weakness of *being* also gets doubled. Strategy and structure move sideways on the HOS toward action and management, and this particular flow is perhaps the one most frequently modeled and expected in the modern workplace. And since it is reinforced, many managers and executive leaders adapt their native flow to mimic this one. The power of this flow is its potential for smart action. The weakness of this flow is the potential disconnect from meaning and relationship.

One of the best skills for leaders in this flow on the OS is to learn the art of asking questions and listening to the answers, rather than coming out of the gate by telling. The connections between logic and action are so clear to the upper quadrant leader that the instinct is to lead by decree; the opportunity is to build teamwork and buy-in through a more collaborative process.

2. Mind to Heart: "Makes sense. But who do I need?"

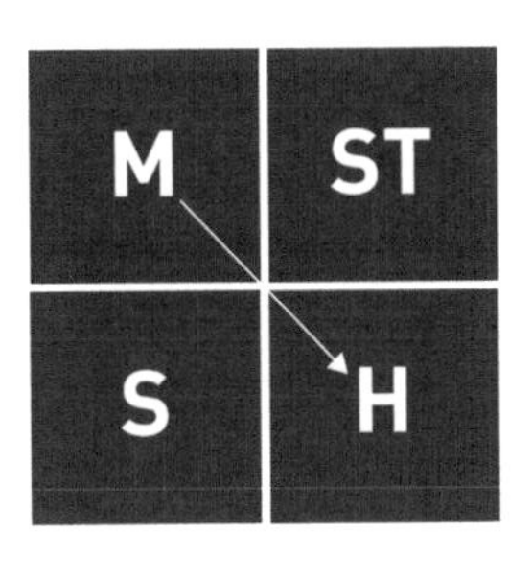

This is an intriguing movement because, like Soul to Strength, it crosses both axes—activating potential from all four sides of the matrix. It begins with strategy and structure and moves instinctively toward teambuilding. It's a move from logic toward relationship, which is an unlikely but extremely rewarding combination. Essentially, these leaders invite a group of people into the world they have designed. The flow combines the superpower of understanding with the superpower of connection.

To hit on all quadrants, Mind to Heart still needs contributions from the Soul-Starter and the Strength-Starter to add vision and purpose from the one, along with data and resources from the other. This unique combination in particular slows down the process or project, yet it gathers a quality of talent and resources that, once it gets pushed into action, is positioned for success.

3. Mind to Soul: "Makes sense. But I need more perspective."

This combination on the HOS stays on the strategic side of the quadrants and, as such, tends to be stronger on conception but weaker on delivery. From a firm grasp on the *What* of the project, it then moves to the *Why* of the project, so the logical-philosophical framework is particularly strong. And the movement from above the line to below is often more accessible to others than the opposite direction, where the Soul-Starter can be clouded in mystery.

This kind of leader begins with designing a product and system and then flows toward seeking a larger perspective in order to understand why it's important and relevant. This is a movement from theory to story, or from the small picture to the big picture. Once the complete picture is understood on both small scale and larger perspective, it's ready to be pushed out to the community for implementation. What Mind to Soul needs from others is to be anchored in team buy-in and delivery.

STRENGTH-STARTERS ON THE MOVE

Strength-Starters are rooted in the capacity for service, so these are your "get-it-done" folks, but then they move to their secondary quadrant to reach for either teamwork (Heart), context (Soul), or strategy (Mind).

1. Strength to Heart: "I'm going to do this. Who's in?"

The Strength to Heart leader is poised and primed to put the project in motion, but these archetypes also know instinctively that without a team standing firmly behind them, the project is dead on arrival. So their natural movement is from activating the plan to gathering support for the plan. This movement carries two implications: by remaining on the tactical side of the quadrants, we know this leader is firmly rooted in the tangibles of people and activity; on the other hand, there is a potential disconnect from the less-tangible commodities of organizational meaning and strategy.

This flow on the HOS is both aggressive and passionate. Leaders in this flow carry a raw power, combining force and feelings in ways that demand a response. They value your contribution on the front lines and genuinely care about you, as long as you're in alignment with the larger mission they are currently on. When Strength-Starters also tap into strategy and meaning, the circle is complete.

2. Strength to Soul: "I'm going to do this. But I wonder why?"

As noted, it takes an unusual leader to cross the axes in both directions with a diagonal flow, but it's a strong movement on the HOS, allowing this type to access all four resources: being, doing, tactical, and strategic. Specifically, Strength to Soul is looking for a larger context that assigns meaning to their activity: a bigger story that places the task or project within a larger vision. The larger vision provides the wisdom to direct the activity on its most effective path.

This archetype combines power and production with meaning and vision. They will need to learn how to care and collaborate, as well as strategize and plan, if they hope to actualize their vision, but a resourced visionary is a rare breed.

3. Strength to Mind: "I'm going to do this. How could it be better?"

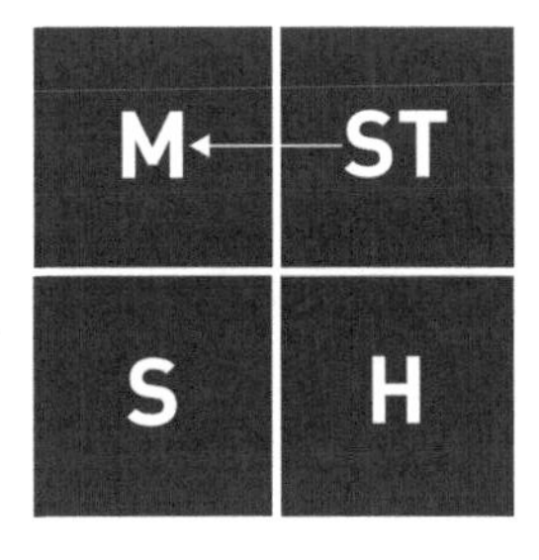

The move from action to strategy allows a good leader to not just rev the engine but also connect that engine to some form of structure or framework for their efforts to scale. When capacity follows courage, this type of person receives the unique advantage to not only see the opportunities for continuous process improvements but to also test and try them out in real time. These are the strategic operators who can slipstream their way up the ranks of organizational hierarchies and are praised for their ability to "kill and drag it home."

After being handed a product to sell, or a project to execute, they are able to leverage existing systems, processes, and structures to maximize their output. They will master a given set of tools to get the job done but will eventually start designing their own as they gain more clarity of the landscape. This type does, however, remain "above the line" for their first two moves, which means that they are susceptible to neglecting or devaluing the Soul and Heart.

By this point, you likely feel an affinity with one or two of the quadrants we've described. Maybe equally valuable, one or two other quadrants feel foreign to you. Life is largely about learning to see yourself deeply and honestly, leading from the fullness of your quadrant capacities and drawing others around you to complement your gifts with theirs.

FINDING AUTHENTICITY

If there is one essential takeaway from this chapter, it's simply this: Take steps in your leadership to know who you are and live out of your True Self. Let's take a cue from Evan Tardy as he describes his personal journey toward authenticity:

When it came to leadership, I was winging it. My team was growing rapidly and looking to me for direction, so I read a bunch of leadership books. But the more I read, the more conflicting information I got, and the more confused I became.

In my work with Transformed Leader, I discovered that I was a chameleon in most of my relationships—trying to adapt to whatever I thought people wanted from me, both at work and at home. As a result, my behavior was inconsistent. Rarely did I feel like I even knew my True Self, and the constant dance among leadership styles was exhausting.

Simply becoming aware of this hidden reflex was illuminating, and it launched my transformational work. I learned that I didn't have to find roles to play as much as live out who I already was. And that I can still be myself while remaining adaptable to different situations, even while harnessing the power of the team around me. As clarity rose, I began to thrive as an executive leader in our organization, and even my personal relationships took on more depth and richness as I began to show up more with my Truer Self.

REFLECTION QUESTIONS

1. *Which "starting block" best represents your innate contribution to your leadership team, and why?*

2. *Which kind of "starter" is most under-represented on your current team, and how might you access that specific skill set?*

3. *Which "on the move" archetype do you resonate most strongly with, and what insights does this offer for your leadership?*

4. *What would it take for you to own your natural starting block and lead with confidence from that position?*

4

WORKING BELOW THE LINE

Harnessing the Transformational Pathway of Change

It had been two full years since Michael lost the lawsuit that damaged his reputation so deeply. He had made business errors — honest mistakes, but damning nonetheless — and the resulting legal liability had cost him dearly. In the aftermath, he struggled with anxiety and depression, obsessing constantly about the pain he had caused his family, friends, and colleagues. He had talked with many about the heavy burden he carried, including pastors and therapists, but he just couldn't let the guilt and shame go. This failure had become an identity of sorts. Even years later, he couldn't find a way to forgive himself and move toward freedom.

Michael joined our monthly leadership cohort, where he quietly participated alongside twelve other business leaders. It was during one of these gatherings when I (Jack) asked him to be the focus of an experiential exercise. The session was titled the "Wisdom of Descent" and was designed to process the leadership failures that all of us experience. In the exercise, Michael worked through three different perceptual positions in the middle of the circle of leaders.

The first was the position of Failure, where Michael proceeded to declare and take ownership of the failure itself and the negative effects that followed it. The second was that of Observer, where he was asked to make his "observations" about the person who failed. Almost always, the reflections of the Observer include strong, emotionally charged judgments about the person who failed. The third and final position is the Grace-Giver, and this is where Michael had the most difficulty. Participants usually need some encouragement to be compassionate and gracious to the parts of themselves that fall short. In Michael's case, he had been punishing himself for so long that he couldn't access any compassion at all for his failure.

In the exercise, I went further to help Michael; I asked him to hold a large rock that symbolized his burden, to hold it out from his body and describe what it felt like to carry it around. He described it as increasingly heavy and tiresome to hold the rock with just his arms. The point was evident: Michael had become spiritually exhausted and emotionally depleted by stewing over his failure. I asked him to keep holding the rock until his arms were trembling and his entire body was experiencing the weight of his shame.

Then I asked the other leaders in the group to put their hands under the rock and lift it up with Michael. For the first time in two years, Michael was able to let go of this defining identity and release the burden he had carried so long. The symbolic act of lifting the rock with the help of other leaders in his community shifted something within him. Michael could finally begin to let the shame go. And from that day forward, he experienced increasing freedom and peace around his failure. Michael's story reminds us of HOS Principle #4: *Leadership growth is catalyzed by a transformational pathway of change.*

Failure is endemic to the human condition. Not only that, but every one of us has to work through the shame of the Shadow Self and the pride of the Ideal Self in order to uncover the True Self with its enduring gifts and authentic contribution. This is the journey toward a happy, healthy life that makes for great leadership over the long haul. This means we have to get good at not only seeing what is true and false about ourselves, but also finding the tools to cultivate a lifestyle of ongoing observation, grace, and growth. In this chapter, we will explore a pathway through the HOS that facilitates integration and transformation.

You have already noticed us talking about working "above the line" and "below the line," referring, of course, to the horizontal axis on the HOS chart: Mind and Strength lie above the line, while Soul and Heart lie beneath. The quadrants above the line prioritize *doing*, while the quadrants beneath prioritize *being*; another way of saying it is that working above the line is primarily externalized, while working beneath the line is primarily internalized. And as we continue to reinforce our approach, effective leadership depends on integrating both in an embodied way.

We do seek, however, to particularly champion work that runs below the line—not because it's more important but because it is frequently ignored and dismissed in our culture, with damaging effect. Figure 4.1 depicts the difference in change potential between learning above the line—primarily focused on cognitive-behavioral change—and the transformational learning that takes place below the line, which involves experiential and symbolic change in the deeper structures of the personality. The circle of trust that surrounds the change process represents the relational context: the only container strong enough to support the transformational leadership journey.

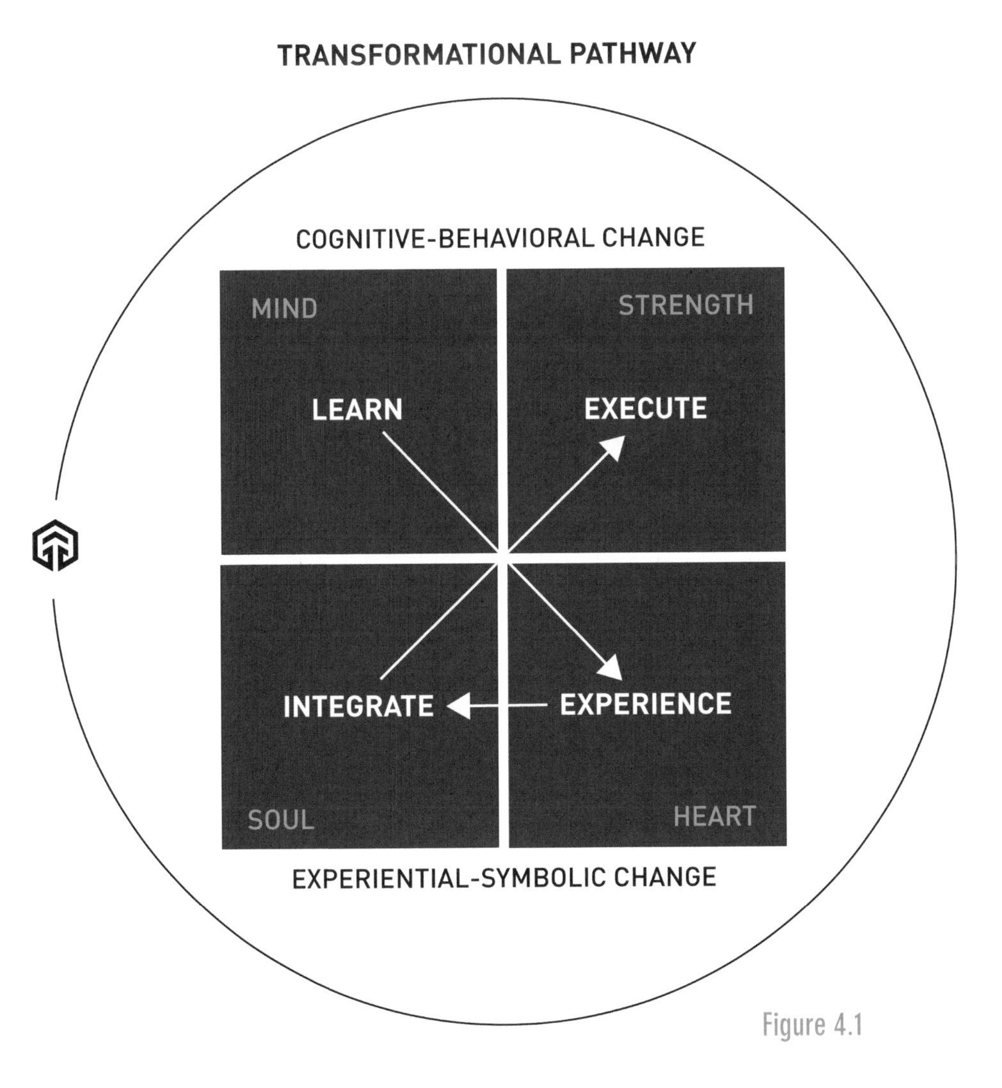

Figure 4.1

The Transformational Pathway is a visual guide on a journey through the quadrants (Mind, Heart, Soul, Strength), where the desired outcome is psychological and spiritual integration. This journey involves engaging the Mind (learning), accessing the Heart (experience), enriching the Soul (integration), and activating one's Strength (execution), all held within a circle of trust. Recent advances in brain research "empirically support the understanding that deep learning follows from cycles of rich sensory experience, reflective meaning interpretation, analytical thought, and directed action."[10] This journey, which we have the opportunity to take at critical times, has the potential to reality-test our meaning perspectives and initiate a structural shift in our assumptions, values, and identities. This pathway offers a template for conversations, meetings, programs, workshops, and other "apps," as we shall see.

LEARN YOUR MEANING PERSPECTIVE

Let's begin by clarifying what we mean when we use the word "transformation." For us, this word denotes a significant change in a person's *meaning perspective* that results in a shift in assumptions, values, or identity.[11] In other words, we all reference the things we value, together with beliefs we assume to be true, to fashion a container for personal identity: *This is what I like, this is what I want, this is the world I live in, and this is who I am in this world.* This combination generates a perspective on reality in the neurological structures of the Mind from which we derive meaning. Or better, we assign meaning and interpret life events based on our perspective. Yet that perspective and assignment of meaning has the potential to change—and needs to change—because our perspectives are never holistic and objective enough to be completely trustworthy. Thus, our need for transformation.

Let's look at this a little closer because this concept is pivotal. We have chosen the term *meaning perspective* to refer to the set of assumptions by which we use our past experiences to assimilate and interpret our new experiences. We don't absorb new experiences from ground zero; we use all our past experiences as points of reference and then use that perspective to filter and assign meaning to what we are experiencing now, as well as what we expect to experience in the future. These frames of reference become for us a (generally unspoken) belief system or worldview for engaging our lives. And this belief system that so deeply filters our life experience can be upgraded through careful work with the HOS. This is what we mean by transformation. It is more than just positive change that comes from the exercise of will. Deep change only occurs when our hidden assumptions and driving values emerge and reorder themselves into a new frame of reference.

EXPERIENTIAL REPATTERNING THROUGH YOUR LEADERSHIP CHALLENGE

This is where our work in the Heart phase really begins at Transformed Leader—when we invite leaders into a group experience based upon their most current leadership challenge, whether that be a business issue, a family responsibility, or a missional endeavor. When high-capacity leaders bring the constant tension of their leadership challenge into an authentic learning community and "work it through" in an open and vulnerable way, the transformational process gains traction.

A four-to-six-month cohort lays the foundation of trust and transparency that allows for the vulnerable Heart work required in this stage of the pathway. Michael's story at the opening of this chapter is an example of how leaders work to name both the external and the internal challenges and resistances, recognize and evaluate the *meaning perspectives* currently in place, and consider new ways to make sense of their past and current journey. This experiential work at the edge of the leader's growth, surrounded by a supportive community of like-minded leaders, forms an alchemy to generate profound insights and emotional breakthroughs. Sooner or later, the ingenuity of the human spirit will surprise and often delight us with a constructive resolution that repatterns the elements of the old *meaning system* and creates a new, more trustworthy point of reference, initiating a new stage of life and leadership. But we're not done yet.

INTEGRATE THE LEARNING UNDER FIRE

The third step on the Transformational Pathway takes us to the Soul, where some of the most challenging work is achieved. The insight or breakthrough obtained in the experiential exercises must now become congruent with the Mind and Heart, resolving the psychological-spiritual split between the light and dark side of the leader's personality. This requires a crucible that can coalesce the internal fragmentation in one's *meaning perspective* toward personal integration and wholeness.

A crucible is a container or melting pot for holding the intense heat and pressure that can transform raw materials and catalytic agents into qualitatively different substances. Many spiritual traditions describe transformation as a process involving severe tests, ordeals, and rites of initiation. Often the metaphors of journey or pilgrimage through the desert are combined with crucible-like images of suffering, testing, and death that leads to rebirth.[12] The intense heat and pressure of resolving one's leadership challenges on this transformational pathway catalyzes deep learning and neurological integration.

Groundbreaking psychologist Daniel Glisczinski offers a heady but incisive perspective on what exactly is taking place in this process:

> Transformative 21st century learning can be constructed by fostering concrete, dissonance-creating experiences that engage multiple senses in learners' brains. Doing so establishes powerful sensory experiences that both register with and yet extend beyond one's existing neuronal networks. In the presence of concrete, experiential cognitive dissonance, learners are ideally positioned to proceed to reflective observation of the multiple, conflicting interpretations that are present in the temporal, associative regions of the brain. Conflicting interpretations become the subjects of critical reflection upon assumptions... and then the transformative learning cycle begins again as committed action situates the learner in the midst of new, novel, increasingly complex and again conflicting concrete experiences.[13]

EXECUTE WITHIN A LEADERSHIP COMMUNITY

The final move on the Transformational Pathway on the HOS is from Soul to Strength, or from meaning to action. Only after having successfully navigated the first three steps can transformational leaders begin to act out of the new learning that has taken place. When high-capacity leaders go below the line and experience the crucible of transformation, then the implementation of the learning is from the inside out and not from the outside in. This is the critical difference between relying upon willpower, a limited resource, and finding energy from the essence of one's being. The outcome of this integrative process is a powerful synergy that will substantially grow a leader's influence.

It is critical that the implementation of experiential learning does not occur in isolation. Transforming leaders need the mentoring, support, and guidance of a circle of trust to internalize the interpretation and validation phase of transformation and sustain deep change in the long run. This calls for an intentional learning community, one that embraces the deep cycle of learning and is committed to this pathway as a lifestyle of leadership. Such a community fosters a culture of change, allowing leaders to safely reflect upon

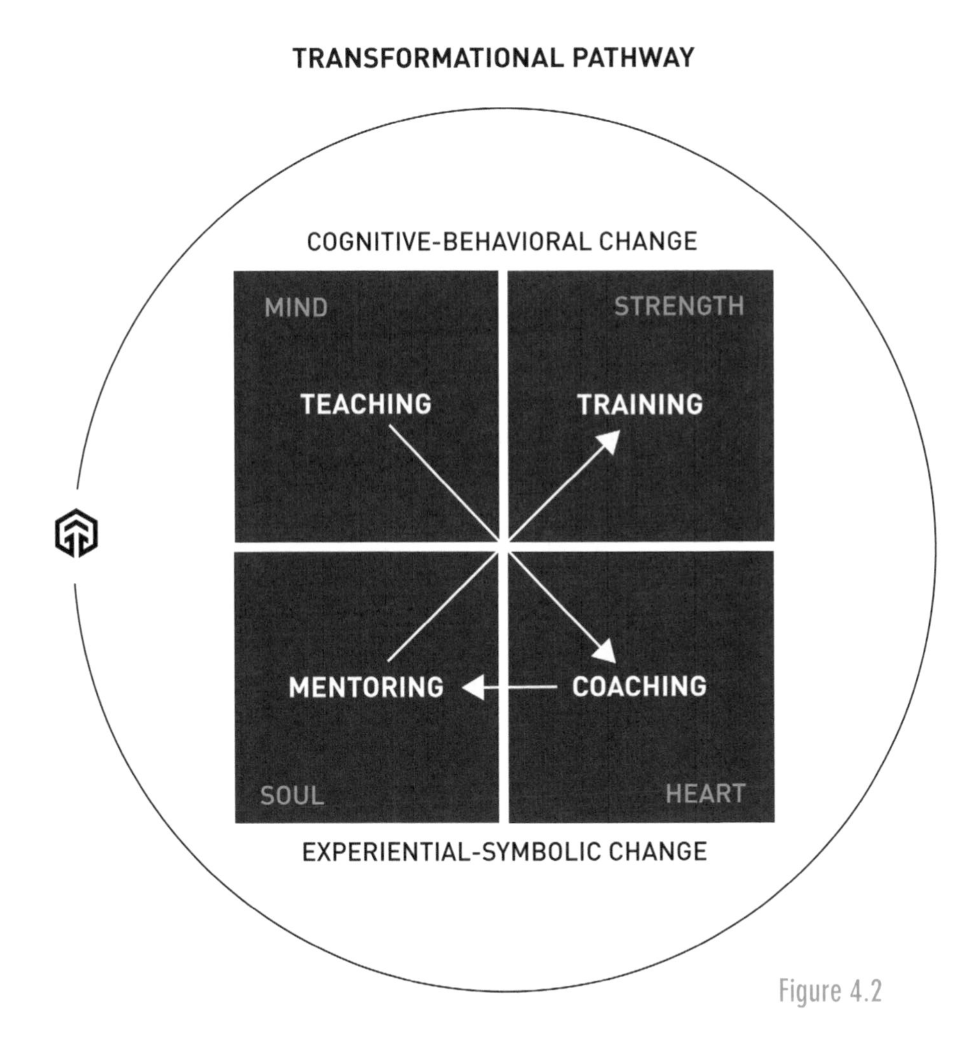

Figure 4.2

the nature and quality of their influence. This circle of trust will be the focus of the next chapter. But first, let's discuss the learning tools associated with the Transformational Pathway.

ACCESSING NEW TOOLS OF INFLUENCE

There are different levels of learning and different tools for influence at each phase of the Transformational Leadership Pathway, and in particular, we want to contrast tools from above the line with tools beneath the line, as seen in Figure 4.2 The movement across the top quadrants from Mind to Strength (cognitive-behavioral change) is very dominant in western culture and can be seen in our educational systems, corporate training programs, military training, therapeutic models, and even non-profit organizations. Contemporary churches or leadership conferences, for example, rely heavily on sitting and listening structures, while neglecting the more transformative approaches to learning that are involved in holistic growth. Elevating reason over experience is one of the tenets of the Enlightenment that continues to affect our practice of human development today.

When leaders are primarily functioning out of the Mind quadrant, they are transferring knowledge, information, and expertise, which is commonly described as *Teaching*. This is an important and necessary activity, but it gets overused in comparison to other, potentially more powerful tools. The same could be said about *Training*, an approach that focuses on skill development in the Strength quadrant, which is very appropriate to the quadrant but limited in transformative impact. Teaching and Training focus almost exclusively on the *doing* side of life, which is why they appeal to the externalized, bottom-line approach of industry. Consequently, these tools of influence fall short of the more comprehensive opportunities beneath the line that address the *being* side of life.

Going below the line into the bottom quadrants activates experiential learning that holds the potential to generate change in meaning, values, and identity, which yields a more enduring formation. This move holds the key to unlock the caliber of leadership that this generation craves most. And this was Michael's experience when he was holding the rock; he crossed the threshold from performance-based worth above the line to that of grace-based worth beneath the line.

The *Coaching* approach to learning is the gift of the Heart quadrant, where the deeper desires of a person—and the values that undergird them—are brought to light for assessment and empowerment. These parts of us tend to remain in the shadows, but transformational coaching has the potential to draw them out and identify resonance or dissonance with behaviors. Similarly, the *Mentoring* approach of the Soul quadrant allows for a life-on-life interplay in relationship that engages the deeper dreams, desires, and destiny of a leader. This is where character and identity are forged, allowing for alignment between the neurological pathways of the Mind and the deeper well of the Soul.

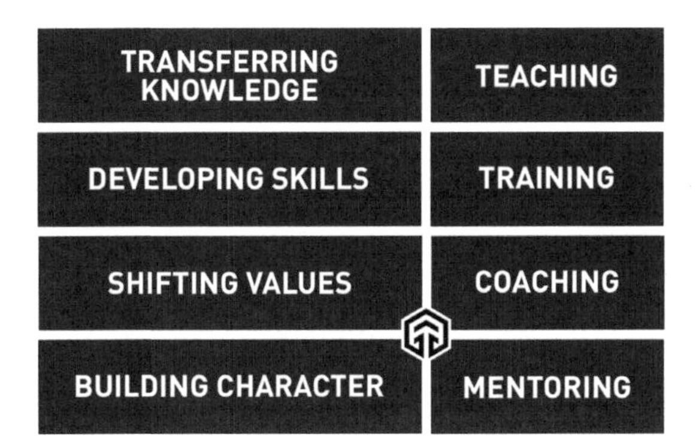

Figure 4.3

By looking at the impact of four learning tools (Figure 4.3), we can see the particular contribution of each. All are useful, but again, we are championing the tools that take people below the line to lay hold of the crucial leadership resources of Heart and Soul. This developmental process happens naturally in healthy marriages and families but rarely takes place in the workplace. The common pushback we encounter is that this level of investment takes too much time and diminishes personal productivity in the short run. Yet, the ROI of leveraging the explosive leadership potential below the line is exponential and positions any enterprise for long-term effectiveness and profitability.

The embodiment of the Transformational Leadership Pathway is a profound challenge for any high-capacity executive. However if leaders aspire to the highest levels of effectiveness and influence, then mastering the art and skill of leading through a transformative interpersonal relationship will become part of their executive skill set. This process can be modeled and multiplied throughout the leaders and teams of the organization, bringing profound improvement in employee satisfaction and productivity. When team members are motivated to give their best and truest selves, it inevitably results in a culture of empowerment.

CROSSING OUR THRESHOLDS

In chapter two, we talked about leadership thresholds. Using the Spiral Diagram, we looked at the big picture "crossings" that define our growth as leaders from authenticity to integration to transformation to transcendence. These are the three overarching transitions that invite us into the full potential of the HOS. These thresholds are just a few of the many we face in our leadership journey.

We could say that *thresholds are central to catalyzing our leadership growth.* Threshold crossings are everywhere, and once we start paying attention to them, we recognize that these opportunities for transition mark us. They invite us out of comfort and complacency into new ways of being. One threshold or another is pretty much staring us in the face at every moment, which means that great leaders are those who get comfortable with change.

In order to cross our thresholds into new levels of maturity and responsibility, aspiring leaders must work through their resistance, tension, and conflict right at the edge of their growth. In the movie *The Matrix*, Neo faced a potent threshold when Morpheus offered him the blue pill or the red pill. Being the seeker he was, Neo took the red pill and crossed the threshold into the horrific reality of the Matrix, but in this new reality, he discovered his true identity, developed his character, and took on the heroic task that embodied his life calling.

Crossing a leadership threshold is difficult and challenging; it requires us to move out of our comfort zone into a space where we cannot control the outcomes. Thresholds challenge a leader's ability to trust that a deeper purpose guides our actions. Crossing a threshold always involves a test of some kind, including, at times, personal suffering—tests that develop and mold a leader's character and prepare him or her for the challenge. Every significant leader, from the biblical Abraham to Abraham Lincoln, from William Wallace to Winston Churchill, have stories of testing that prepared them for a major turning point in history.

In the darkest hours of the Nazi invasion of France, Churchill was appointed prime minister of England and took on the responsibility of protecting his homeland from the armies of Adolf Hitler. As he went to bed at 3:00

a.m. on May 11, 1940, Churchill journaled that he felt as if he were walking with destiny, and that all his past life had simply been preparation for that hour and that trial. Not all thresholds reach the magnitude of spearheading national struggles for survival, but they do have common characteristics that arise when men and women engage the Transformational Leadership Pathway. Leaders who resolve to walk and lead others along this path must overcome Resistance, Shadow, and Shame as thresholds to growth (Figure 4.4)

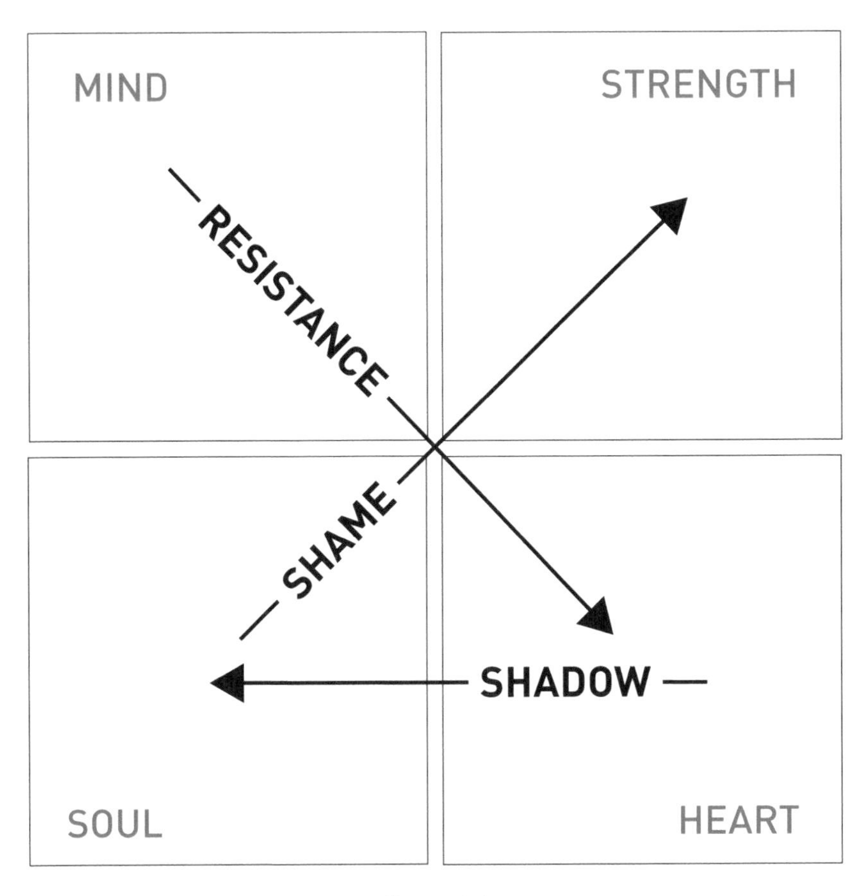

Figure 4.4

Resistance: Crossing from Mind to Heart

When leaders aspire to grow beyond their current capacity, they experience resistance because the *structural mind* fights for stability and order, while the *survival heart* will be threatened by disruptive change. We typically experience this threat with the familiar reflexes of fight, flight, or freeze. Many of us will then avoid processing the painful emotions of fear, doubt, and anxiety and play it safe, staying where it feels familiar and avoiding the challenge that stretches us beyond our current capacities. But if we can summon our courage right at this threshold and work through the resistance, the gold of personal integration and wholeness lies right on the other side.

The willingness to reflect upon our primal emotions and process them within relationships of trust allows greater awareness and confidence to take hold in the conscious mind. The empathy we receive from a trusted relationship is critical to working through our resistance. This can be a mentor, a counselor, a wise friend, a trusted advisor, or a loving spouse, but the decisive step revolves around our vulnerability. The risk to move beyond fear with a safe companion propels us across this threshold and into the next stage.

Shadow: Crossing from Heart to Soul

Once we've overcome our resistance to change, the next leadership threshold to cross is to *own our shadow*. Getting in touch with the Heart in the midst of a threatening leadership challenge exposes both the light and dark sides of our leadership. The natural tendency of our Ideal Self is to embrace the light side and disown the shadowy parts, the parts we disdain and find embarrassing. We don't want to look weak or out of control, so we project our Ideal Selves in the midst of disruptive change rather than lead with authenticity. While this is instinctive and normal, it's also counterproductive. The very process of integration we seek is disrupted when we repress our Shadow Self.

In David McCullough's tome, *1776*, he describes the terrifying fear that George Washington experienced when the Revolutionary War seemed completely hopeless. Washington shared his profound angst in personal correspondence with friends he could trust. He didn't hide from his shadow but processed his fears through writing, expressing the darkest parts of his inner life. Shadow work allowed Washington to process his terrible dread and then find the internal resolve to lead his troops into courageous confrontations.[14]

The paradox here is that the more we own our shadow material, the more it loses its latent power. When we can be honest with ourselves about the possibility of being corrupt, manipulative, controlling, and even vengeful, the less these parts take over and control us. Exposing the darker passions of the Heart to the light of our awareness and spiritual insight activates healing and reconciliation in the Soul. Often the shadow side of our leadership is not necessarily bad or evil, just unknown. Sometimes it requires a daunting challenge to reveal parts of the Soul that have never been embraced or integrated into the whole. When the shadow is seen as a messenger rather than an enemy, one can actually be curious and learn what it has to teach us. Executives who own and integrate their shadows are more authentic, resonant leaders than those who repress their shadow in order to perform.

Shame: Crossing from Soul to Strength

Transcending our pride and shame is the fundamental challenge of being fully human. This is especially true when we cross the leadership threshold from shadow work to *actually own our power*. Pride tempts us to promote our self-image and to rely on charisma and willpower to surmount great challenges. Shame, on the other hand, is the feeling of emptiness or unworthiness that generates reluctance to lead. The image-bound leader is reluctant to cross the threshold of Soul to Strength for fear of being found out. Performing to maintain a projected image is vastly different than embracing and expressing the essence of a leader's Soul.

In the Academy Award-winning movie, *Chariots of Fire*, Olympic runners Eric Liddell and Harold Abrahams represented very different ways a person can own his or her power. Abrahams was a Jewish outsider at the class-conscious University of Cambridge, while Eric Liddell was a devout Scottish Christian preparing to serve as a missionary in China. They both won Gold Medals at the 1924 Olympics, but they ran for different reasons. Abrahams ran as an expression of racial defiance, while Liddell ran from the sheer joy of it. Eric owned his legitimate power with the famous line, "God has made me fast, and when I run, I feel his pleasure."

Having worked with driven, high-capacity leaders for many years, we have learned that *self-image undermines true self-esteem*. When leaders detach in order to perform, they try to change things from the outside-in (self-image); however, when leaders perform out of their Soul or essence, there is congruence in their performance from the inside-out (self-esteem). When Liddell won the Gold Medal in the 400 meters, he was performing at the highest levels, while being true to his Soul. He was able to cross the threshold of Shame to own his authentic power as a mature man and leader.

CONVICTION, COURAGE, & COMMITMENT

The invitation to cross leadership thresholds has a way of raising internal resistance for many, so it bears mention what some of those resistances might be so we can anticipate and overcome them. For starters, a leader, team, or organization may buy into the idea of a new leadership paradigm—and even the importance of going beneath the line—but only tease the idea, rather than fully commit to it. It's smart to test new ideas, but the incredible potential of installing the HOS will only be fully realized with a deep commitment to its implementation over the long run.

Any leader who has been around the block has seen new ideas float into an organization, then float back out after a period of time. New leadership concepts, paradigms, or ideas are plentiful and exciting, fostering a corporate culture full of innovative philosophies and concepts. Still, environments need to be cultivated or processes begun that can nurture these seeds. Deeper change initiatives are even more challenging to embrace and implement. Suppose decision-makers do not wholeheartedly commit to them. In that case, it becomes nearly impossible to maintain traction in light of how much time, energy, and commitment is required to see them through. Furthermore, transformative change can be more invasive and uncomfortable, that makes it understandable for a leader, team, or organization to revert towards the approaches and strategies they are most familiar with or comfortable employing.

Another obstacle to transformative change arises when a leader decides to go below the line to deepen his or her leadership without getting buy-in from powers higher up the line. The effort defaults to a personal initiative rather than a company-wide initiative, which can in turn threaten senior leaders and generate resistance. The personal investment in your leadership development is still worth it, but keep in mind that senior leaders who have not done their own work below the line, nor want to, may respond by sidelining or silencing those who do.

There is also the reality that many leaders are so perpetually harried and overwhelmed that they don't have the bandwidth or interest in trying anything new. It's survival mode, pure and simple. In this cultural quagmire, the stability of the status quo is clung to tenaciously, and change is resisted vigorously. A leader must have vision, courage, and commitment to work for transformative change, and that takes a high level of conviction. Our goal in this chapter, and the book at large, is to cast a vision compelling enough to be worthy of your effort to instigate these kinds of changes, then enjoy the fruit of your labors. We don't take that trust lightly and wouldn't tease you with false hope if we had not experienced the massive benefits, in ourselves and so many of our clients.

REFLECTION QUESTIONS

1. *How is your life and leadership becoming fragmented right now? How will you move toward more integration, wholeness, and psychological maturity?*

2. *To what extent do you rely upon willpower to execute your leadership roles and responsibilities? What would it be like for you to tap into your soul for a deeper source of presence and power?*

3. *What is it like for you to face your own shadow? How do you process the dark side of your leadership when it reveals itself in your thoughts, feelings, or behavior?*

4. *What keeps you from owning your legitimate power? How do you intend to overcome the limitations of pride and shame in order to function as a transformative leader?*

5

STRENGTHENING THE CIRCLE

Nurturing Trust in Community

April 3, 2019, was a wild day for the history books. It's a day that completely changed my life.

One minute, I (Rob) was a competent, collected person leading a transformational cohort with a group of executive leaders, and an hour later, I was not. Dazed and confused, I couldn't remember the last few hours. Miraculously, I picked up the cell phone when my wife called from California to check in from her travels, and she knew immediately that something was terribly wrong. Even now, I have no real memory of that day or the days that followed, but what I do know is that a host of trusted friends rushed to my side as I was wheeled into the hospital while I was stuck in a two-minute conversation loop that lasted close to two days.

"Where am I? How did I get here? What happened? Where is Natalie? Where are the kids? I'm so scared." Question, question, question, repeat. I am also told I said other funny, scary, honest, and inappropriate things. I am choosing to plead the fifth, and I can, therefore, neither confirm nor deny these claims.

I had experienced a stroke. Five actually, from what they can tell by the scarred tattoos of trauma that are forever etched on my brain. Apparently, two injured blood vessels on the back of my neck had been the culprits for causing all this fuss—a ticking bomb that finally exploded. In the last year since that moment, there has been much to celebrate and much to grieve.

"Dad, you're different now. It's been hard to get to know and be with this new you, but I would rather have a different dad than no dad at all."

It was hard to hear that from one of my children at the one-year anniversary mark. And it's true: I am a different person, and there's no going back. I've had to renegotiate all my meaningful relationships in the year since. Some friends have drifted away, feeling unsure about how to be with Rob 2.0, while others have reaffirmed their place in my life with renewed affection and perseverance.

I had spent most of my life trying to prove that I could exceed everyone's expectations and claw my way to the top of the heap. Now I was coming to terms with a new normal—that only some of my previous capacities would be replaced slowly over time. The stroke has forced me to redefine success, and I'm learning to measure it now, not just in outcomes, but also in terms of the important people in my life.

And of the many things I've learned from that unexpected trauma, this is the most profound: The *who* you walk life with matters far more than *what* you accomplish. If you have solid people at your side, it enriches and compounds the potential for a deeper, more meaningful life. Many friends came to visit me as the crisis broke. Many sat with me, stayed with me, listened to me, fed me, and even clothed me. How can you repay such depth of relationship? Perhaps we're not meant to think like that. Deep relationships become less about keeping score and more about holding intentionality with one another in the foreground.

I believe that, together with those who continue to invest in my life, I can stumble my way forward into a more beautiful, sacred life. I hope that you, too, count yourself wealthy in the quality of friendships you hold dear, even though most leaders I know struggle to count close friends on one hand. It's our hope that this chapter will help equip you for the great quest that we call HOS Principle #5: *Leadership growth deepens within relationships of trust.*

The most critical factor in effective leadership today is building relationships of trust. Rarely do leaders succeed without the loyalty, support, and trust of their colleagues and followers. Many leaders are also profoundly isolated in their roles and have difficulty sustaining deep friendships. It is imperative that we learn how to forge and nurture relationships of trust that can provide the friendship, support, and development we need to function and grow as leaders.

THE LONELINESS PANDEMIC

We are now familiar with the unprecedented social upheaval of the COVID-19 virus which tore a wide swath across our world in 2020. And not unlike recovery from a stroke, it takes longer than expected to find a new normal.

At the same time, there is a much quieter pandemic that has crept silently through the ranks of our global community in recent years with little notice or care: *loneliness.* The last few decades have exponentially expanded our ability to connect casually with thousands of clients and contacts literally around the globe with the push of a button. Instant messaging, instant audio, instant video—and it's mostly free. These advancements have also driven the concept of building personal online platforms that can be used to further leverage our brands, our ideas, our businesses, and along with those, our Ideal Selves. Yet for all that, we, as a generation, are increasingly lonely.

Perhaps we have traded deeper connection for more contacts. The casualty is interpersonal communion.

Loneliness, fueled by the industrial revolution and subsequent movements, has become firmly rooted in our organizations and institutions, where people are commonly reminded to check their personal problems at the door. As a result, leaders have lost any real place to have meaningful relationships that can support, encourage, nurture, and care for their growth and development. The conversation about loneliness has swelled in recent years, highlighted in a 2010 study by psychology and epidemiology researchers who demonstrated that being lonely did as much physical damage to our bodies as "smoking fifteen cigarettes a day, and was more predictive of early death than the effects of air pollution or physical inactivity."[15] Perhaps it's fair to say we have become chain-loners, rather than chain-smokers.

And a recent study published in the *Harvard Business Review* found that workers who experienced higher levels of loneliness also reported fewer promotions, less job satisfaction, and a greater frequency in job change. Moreover, the study tagged lawyers, doctors, and engineers as the occupations reporting the highest levels of loneliness, suggesting a connection between the proportion of time spent at work and the feeling of isolation and alienation.[16]

Social commentator Robert Bly reflects on our current crisis, particularly among men, in this way: "Contemporary business life allows competitive relationships only, in which the major emotions are anxiety, tension, loneliness, rivalry, and fear."[17]

The loneliness pandemic is compounded by the dynamic we have written about throughout the book: the workplace culture is dominated by an overemphasis on the upper quadrants of Mind and Strength to the almost complete neglect of Heart and Soul. This means that you are expected to be fully focused during your 40–60 hours a week at work, generating profitable outcomes. Relationships are completely utilitarian, and workers know full well they are expendable. Depth of meaning and connection are luxuries we simply can't afford in the economic pressure to stay ahead of the competition, yet the toll that loneliness takes on us is more than emotional. A handful of social prophets such as Patrick Lencioni have been tracking the impact of relational disengagement on the bottom line of the financial statement.[18] The long-term consequences of this pandemic, if left unaddressed, will be dire for the marketplace.

Just last month, we personally encountered two organizations that fell apart because of the isolation and eventual implosion of the primary leader. For decades, these executives had managed and concealed parts of their humanity that were unwelcome in the organizational culture. For both, the dam eventually burst to the surprise of even their closest colleagues. Our modern business culture has tremendous power to isolate and silence the emotional problems of leaders.

We also observe the toxic effects of the traditional organizational pyramid that continues to prop up a dysfunctional, hierarchical approach to executive leadership, even when the dehumanizing effects of such structures have been known for decades. While a single perch at the top allows for faster decisions, that agility brings with it the very real threat of skewed perspective and corruption that can damage both leader and institution. Further, a hierarchical approach "nourishes the notion among people that one must be the boss to be effective."[19] Leadership consultant Robert Greenleaf goes on to observe that "we have too few [leaders] because most institutions are structured so that only a few—only one at the time—can emerge" and this limits the full scope of leadership to just one person, no matter how big the organization.[20] These are just a sampling of the corporate maladies that trace themselves back to the fundamental problem of leadership loneliness. What can be done about it?

TRUST CIRCLES

For those looking to turn the tide with us, we have established, both academically and experientially, that leadership growth deepens and accelerates within relationships of trust. One of the ways we are fighting the tide of relational marginalization at Transformed Leader is by guiding leaders to establish personal and professional Trust Circles. These relational collaborations provide exceptional spaces to not only rebuild the qualities of Heart and Soul that the modern workplace needs so desperately, but also provide for the deeper changes and integration that impact attitudes, behaviors, and contributions.

So, what is a Trust Circle? It's a small group in which leaders bring together a committed "band of brothers or sisters" to meet periodically for focused work on the Transformational Pathway (chapter four). Trust Circles, whether personal or professional, are where holistic leadership can be embodied, not just studied, on the journey to becoming an Authentic Leader, an Integrated Leader, a Transformational Leader, and ultimately, a Transcendent Leader (chapter two). Leaders on this journey become fully aware of both their competencies and their limitations. Specifically, they come to accept limitations as a gift that invites them into community with others—safe communities, where members are embraced and supported in their entirety. Where transparency and support create a formative environment leading to creative solutions to complex systemic problems.

Deep change happens best when built upon relationships of trust. This should be on every leader's radar. Who do you trust most with the messier parts of your life? *Do you actually go there?* Leaders who want to carry transformative influence must establish intentional relationships in their personal and professional contexts in order to strengthen the foundation of their own personhood so their influence can be, in fact, trusted. A solid Trust Circle is where the unique story of each person is heard, valued, and redeemed by the mysterious healing power of the community.

There is an ancient Greek word for encouragement (*parakaleo*) that describes the critical factor that strengthens people in their ongoing struggle with life. When someone cares enough to "come alongside" you, as this word suggests, and is committed to being with you through your struggle—that is when you will feel real hope, support, and encouragement. This ancient truth is now being affirmed by modern science.

THE NEUROLOGY OF CHANGE

As you may have noticed, the field of neurobiology has been taking huge strides in recent years, particularly as it relates to the plasticity of the mind. Plasticity and transformation are two sides of the same coin: one is the scientific perspective, while the other is the socio-spiritual perspective.

Daniel Siegel has made the case through his work as a clinical professor of psychiatry at the UCLA School of Medicine and executive director of the Mindsight Institute that relationships and the brain interact to shape who we are. He argues that it is impossible for us to change or transform outside of interpersonal relationships that revolve around trust. "Through understanding the connections between mental processes and brain functioning, we can build a neurobiological foundation for the ways in which interpersonal relationships—both early in life and throughout adulthood—continue to play a central role in shaping the emerging mind."[21]

Psychologist Sue Johnson concurs: "Our biggest need is for safe connection, especially with one or two people whom we feel loved by, and to not understand how crucial this connection is as a resource is costing us plenty. When you get people together and help them feel safe and open up these channels of communication, they become better at everything. This is not just me talking; it's the research. This is science, not sentiment. Safe connection is powerful wherever you have it, even outside of the home. Can you become a better team member? Can you collaborate? Can you coordinate with people, or are you always defensive and trying to get ahead? With trusted connections, we become better at solving problems, collaborating, and everything else. It's really time we start to get this!"[22]

STORY AS CHANGE AGENT

Brain science also speaks to the transformative power of storytelling, which is located in the Soul quadrant. Paul Zak researched the power of story to affect attitudes, beliefs, and behaviors through the release of oxytocin in the brain. The data demonstrated that powerful stories motivate social reciprocity by gathering attention and emotional resonance. Great stories have staying power through one's identification with the characters—a bond that has the potential to move us to action.[23]

It is no secret that stories are important. What has been lost in our culture, however, is the sharing of stories within the context of the Trust Circle. Trust is the active ingredient that takes story beyond the transactional delivery of a keynote presentation, a book, or generalized conversation to the transformational context of mutual vulnerability and internal movement. This movement expands exponentially to impact not only the one who is sharing but also those who are listening. Story and connection can motivate men and women to face their leadership challenges with more courage and boldness.

When leaders feel safe enough within the community, they are more open to sharing the authentic parts of their story, even the parts that feel dangerous, which invites listeners to connect to the feelings behind the words. Then the personal, collective, and shared experiences within a Trust Circle create narrative arcs and storylines that are compelling for the entire group, potentially unlocking possibilities for an entire organizational culture. Within the strong container of trusted relationships, community learning transcends individual learning, allowing for deep simultaneous change across a group. The personal stories and experiences of each leader are swept up in a larger, more redemptive narrative.

Jason Walch says it this way: "Narratives—their appeal to interest, their intersubjectivity, and their call upon imagination, making them coherent and significant—offer a 'fast pass' to our cognitive belief system . . . Narratives give to us a sensible and meaningful account of the experience of others, and likewise, help us to make sense and meaning of our experiences. Our view of the world—or cognitive belief system—takes on the texture of the most meaningful narratives we have encountered or directly experienced."[24]

Knowing that trusted community is hard to find but essential to growing our leadership authentically, Transformed Leader has pioneered several group and cohort settings that have established a solid track record in facilitating the transformational pathway. We have watched leaders change before our eyes into authentic, integrated change agents, and this powerful work has satisfied a lifelong dream.

As a teenager, I (Rob) remember making a deal with a few friends that we would never grow up to be as lonely and isolated as the older men we saw in our community. We couldn't understand why these forty- and fifty-somethings seemed so detached and alone. Their faces were blank and dull, and it seemed they had lost all sense of fun and genuine community; all they did was work. Together, we pledged to never become like them.

Now in my forties and an adult myself, married, studying, parenting, and working, I carry more compassion for those leaders, having experienced firsthand the challenges of growing up in our current culture. Deep meaningful relationships are extremely hard to forge and sustain in the midst of all the pressures of life. Everyone and everything is pulling on us to erode meaningful interpersonal communion.

Let's get supremely practical about this. Now is the time to look at the particulars of creating your personal and professional Trust Circles.

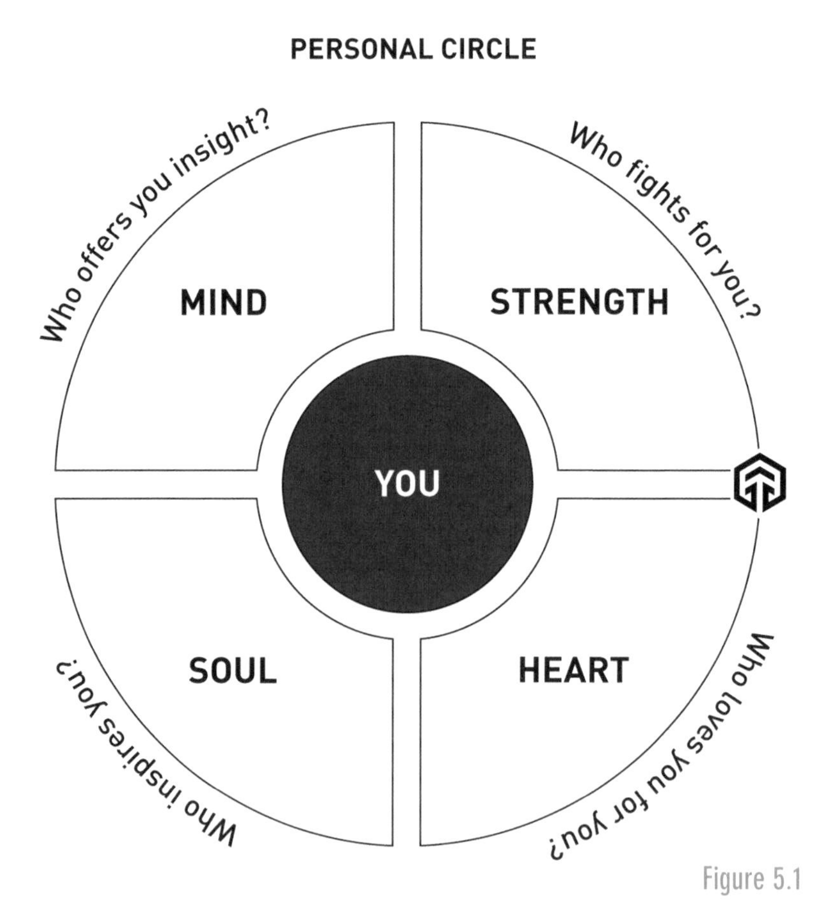

Figure 5.1

YOUR PERSONAL CIRCLE

The Personal Circle is an intentional gathering of people who have already invested in your life to the extent that trust has been established. Who fights for you, offers wisdom and perspective, just loves you for you, and brings strategic insight? Or who do you sense has that strong potential and would be willing to invest the time and commitment? This will become a resourcing team that can underpin your development more than you could ever do alone.

What you are looking for specifically is at least four personal allies that represent some or all of the quadrants on the HOS. We've already established the depth of what the Heart-Starter, the Soul-Starter, the Mind-Starter, and the Strength-Starter have to offer, so this is your chance to move purposefully and actively to draw upon the wisdom of each quadrant and apply it to your personal leadership journey. The Personal Circle is carefully designed to help you take stock of your life, recognize the wonders and shadows you carry, and to energize your mission, purpose, and calling as you become a leader of destiny.

As you consider who belongs in your Circle, here are the more particular questions to ask:

1. Who loves you for you?

These are the Heart-Starters—those who express a deep sense of love and care for you. They love and like you in ways that seem to transcend what you know or how you perform. They simply see you and want to be with you. They carry a depth of affection and commitment that offers a sense of true belonging and helps you believe in yourself.

2. Who inspires you?

These are the Soul-Starters—those who bring a grand perspective, depth, and meaning to your life. They may be in their fifties, sixties, seventies, or beyond: They have seen enough life and done enough of their own integrative work below the line to speak from the deep wisdom and inspiration of a sage.

3. Who gives you insight?

These are your Mind-Starters—those who intuitively carry a structural perspective on the world and have the capacity to provide a strategic overview of your challenges and opportunities. These individuals are likely in their forties or fifties, so they have a wealth of experience that can resource your own.

4. Who fights for you?

These are your Strength-Starters—those who carry enormous energy and passion for getting things done. This is the warrior in your life who shows up, no questions asked, sword in hand, ready to fight to the death alongside you in whatever way you need. Sometimes this ally is a little younger—thirties or forties—and brings a catalytic power to your life.

FIVE CIRCLE COMPONENTS

There are five potential components to constructing a Personal Circle: the Roundtable, Mentoring and Coaching, Peer Support and Friendship, an Integration Project, and a Retreat. Each brings its own formative potential to the Circle, but the Roundtable is the hub. Some Personal Circles may go no further than this and still experience tremendous benefit.

It is important to share the nature, boundaries, and expectations of your Personal Circle so those who are invited clearly understand what you are asking of them. We also suggest that you invite people outside your direct work environment to allow for more autonomy and privacy when you bring professional challenges to the group, not needing to be overly cautious with potential career blowback or power dynamics. You will probably want to limit your invitations to locals, which allows these components to converge practically, but you can get creative. We have various helpful outlines, templates, and guidance to help leaders activate and then manage their Circle, but here are the five main components to consider as you build your team.

1. The Roundtable

The Roundtable forms the official gathering of the Circle, which usually takes place for three hours (usually during the evening) three or four times a year. We suggest a one- or two-year commitment from those you invite into your Personal Circle. The Roundtable offers the opportunity to not only connect and bond over a meal but also to bring your leadership challenges and updates to the group for the purpose of harvesting the perspectives, advice, encouragement, and guidance of your Circle.

2. Mentoring and Coaching

The Roundtable itself offers fragments of organically prompted mentoring and coaching, but we suggest you informally instigate one-on-one meetings outside this setting, where the leader purposefully engages certain individuals in the Circle to seek out more of this interaction. For me (Rob), this looks like regularly resourcing some of the older men in my Circle over lunch or coffee to ask for specific, direct coaching or mentoring around a certain topic.

3. Peer Support and Friendship

Peer support and friendship are vital, and we assume that everyone in your Personal Circle is a friend to some degree. The potential of gleaning the benefits as a person and a leader is leveraged in enjoyable ways by hardwiring intentional touchpoints throughout the year with everyone at your table. Having fun and chasing adventure with others allows relationships to deepen naturally, and this in turn adds value back to the Roundtable.

4. An Integration Project

The integration project is a component that should be identified and designed around a leader's particular leadership challenge or goals. It is a personal initiative selected and driven by the leader but resourced and supported by the Circle. An integration project could be a leader's failing marriage, an addiction, the loss of a loved one, a parenting crisis, or an expanded job role or career change, for example. After clarifying the challenge, the group is there to help the individual outline his or her project and then walk alongside that person as he or she engages it over a specific period of time.

5. Retreats

Hosting an annual retreat with your Personal Circle can be a powerful time to maximize connection and cultivate more depth and synergy within the team. These retreats combine adventure, friendship, and structure to deepen your relationships outside of the normal routines of life. We find that powerful opportunities naturally emerge when you get outside your normal life context for one or more days.

You can probably visualize how some combination of these five elements, anchored in a Roundtable gathering every three to four months, has the potential to enrich your life and leadership in ways we rarely access otherwise. We can certainly say that these components have enriched our personal development as leaders, and we've observed the same for others who have engaged in this endeavor. In fact, we would say it even stronger than that: No other application within the HOS has greater transformative potential than Trust Circles. The process of proactively culling the unique contributions of quadrants outside our own makes for dramatic impact on our growth—a caliber of personal development that simply does not occur otherwise.

TRANSFORMATIVE TEAMS

Similar to your Personal Circle, we suggest you extend some of these same ideas and concepts to bring more focus and intentionality around empowering the effectiveness of your team. Transformational leaders seeking to disrupt and catalyze their organization, and even their industry, have to think strategically and know how to get the right people positioned and aligned with one another.

We developed the Transformative Teams framework (Figure 5.2) for resourcing high-functioning teams within an organization. By understanding the four primary leadership styles that flow from the quadrants, you will be equipped to not only identify your own natural strengths in your leadership role, but also identify others who can bring their essential perspectives for the ultimate purpose of resourcing, informing, and guiding leadership decisions.

A team like the one we are proposing carries high emotional intelligence, the capacity for informing crucial conversations, and transforming conflict into constructive energy. These organizational resources are, quite simply, priceless.

TRANSFORMATIVE TEAMS

MIND

STRATEGIC LEADERSHIP

Effective Policies
Standardized procedures
Clear Roles & Responsibilities

Aligned Structures
Common Assumptions
Unifying Beliefs

What is the **framework** of our enterprise?

STRENGTH

OPERATIONAL LEADERSHIP

Superior Execution
Benchmark Practices
Measurable & Attainable Goals

Interdependent Systems
Power Incentives
Excellent Service

How do we **perform** as an enterprise?

SOUL

VISIONARY LEADERSHIP

Compelling Vision
Innovative Processes
Creative Ideas

Iconic Brands
Meaningful Symbols
Core Story

What gives **meaning** to our enterprise?

HEART

COLLABORATIVE LEADERSHIP

Shared Values
Skilled Communication
Emotional Intelligence

Invested Stakeholders
Relationships of Trust
Collaboraitve Community

How do we **relate** as an enterprise?

Figure 5.2

During the upcoming section, consider which of these four leadership styles, or competencies, resonate most strongly for you and which are more challenging to access. There is generally a correlation between your quadrant of origin and your leadership style. The qualities that make you a Strength-Starter, for example, are usually the same qualities that position you uniquely as an Operational Leader, although you doubtless have to draw upon strategic, visionary, and collaborative elements at times.

This understanding alone is often the outcome of lengthy and expensive consultations with experts, but you can probably answer this question within minutes. As you do, begin to consider where those on your team would land. It's common to attract or hire others who are similar to us, but high-functioning teams consist of individuals centered around a shared vision who provide complementary leadership contributions. A healthy enterprise requires teams who bring strategic, collaborative, visionary, and operational intelligence and expertise. We often intuit this on a conceptual level, yet few leaders know what to do about it or have a simple tool like our Transformative Teams framework to guide the process. It is vital that these styles are identified within a team to ensure that all bases are covered or inform potential reshuffling or resourcing for that to be accomplished.

We worked with a team of executive leaders from an organization not long ago. After describing the four primary leadership styles necessary for an integrated team, we asked them to go stand in the quadrant that felt most like "home" for each of them. The idea was that the quadrants related to their leadership style and most significant contributions. The general manager identified himself as an operational leader; two others stood in the strategic leadership quadrant; and the last one selected collaborative leadership. The exercise became an instant visual for the four of them.

While collectively aligned by organizational vision and mission, they were individually scattered across the room based on their unique gifting and leadership contributions within that higher purpose. It also became strikingly clear that the Visionary Leadership quadrant was lonely and vacant. We discussed how they could resource one another better to become more integrated as a team. Also, they would need to ensure that Visionary Leadership attributes like meaning, innovation, and creativity would not be neglected within their own unit, leaving them limited and ineffective.

Let's unpack these leadership gifts a bit further to help you become more informed as you consider those in your team.

FOUR PRIMARY LEADERSHIP STYLES

1. The Collaborative Leader

The Collaborative Leader is motivated by the desires and values of the Heart. Relationships are primary, and this is what fundamentally guides his or her decisions. These leaders demonstrate keen emotional intelligence and can easily read the relational dynamics and tensions in the room. This is a strength but can also turn to a weakness if Collaborative Leaders get enmeshed in relationships without healthy boundaries or withdraw from conflict. Their natural empathy makes them excellent communicators and mediators in other people's conflicts. They are especially effective at leading teams and building an inclusive, productive, empowering culture in their work environments. Unfortunately, Collaborative Leaders are often the least valued executive in a typical business enterprise.

Collaborative Leaders have a significant opportunity in your Professional Circle to evaluate and assess how your decisions are being made and whether that process is complementing the growth, performance, and health of the enterprise. Dennis Bakke, founder and former CEO of the AES Corporation, developed a distributed decision-making process designed to unlock the potential of everyone within the organization. Bakke's motivations would tag him to the gift-mix of a Collaborative Leader. He outlined core problems that he believes lead to an unengaged workforce—an internal threat that can ultimately harm the entire organization. His collaborative model challenged the ruling assumption that it's the "higher-ups" in position and power who are most qualified to make the important decisions of a company and assigned fresh value to the larger sphere.[25] Such is the gift of the Heart-based leader; it's the glue that forges powerful bonds to unify and resource an enterprise.

Who are the people on your team or in your organization that embody the traits of a Collaborative Leader?

2. The Visionary Leader

The Visionary Leader is motivated by what gives meaning and purpose to an enterprise. They bring to your team an ability to provide keen insight into what others do not see—helping you find a compelling vision and story within the organization. When they function in their strengths, they weave a powerful narrative that unites people around a common purpose. The Visionary Leader understands that the workplace environment is like almost everything else—a moving target that requires agility and re-calibration, and they undergird these moments with a steady conviction for the underlying mission. These men and women invest time to reflect on their own calling and unique contribution, the grand perspectives that govern the context, and the unseen unconscious cultural currents at play in the industry.

All executive leaders are expected to carry and deliver vision, whether it comes naturally to them or not, and it's important to note that the attribute of vision has become widely admired and emulated in our current culture. Yet while many have learned to package foresight as vision, it may not be a true embodiment of this style if it is not accessing the Soul as its source. Such "vision" is more of a mental construct than a meaning construct and flows more from the Head than the Soul. In contrast, a true Visionary Leader sees the future needs of an organization and then navigates beyond that target to address shifting values, identities, and paradigms—the elements that ground vision in meaning.

The shadow side of this leadership style is manipulation, using creative capacity and symbology to control instead of authentically care for others. Visionary Leaders often have difficulty with the execution and implementation of tasks. The ability to perceive the big picture and inspire direction may give way to disinterest when it comes to managing the steps necessary for execution. Their value is immense, however, because without Visionary Leadership, there is no compelling *Why* behind the *What* and *How* of an enterprise. When such leaders pair their intuitive insights with the connectivity of the Heart or the logic of the Mind, the leadership team can begin considering what the best next structures, practices, and culture should be to actualize the vision, and this is the treasure that the Visionary brings to your team.

Who are the people on your team or in your organization that embody the traits of a Visionary Leader?

3. The Strategic Leader

The Strategic Leader is a builder and brings to your team a dexterity for establishing viable structures, effective policies, and conceptual frameworks—

foundational insights to help your enterprise thrive. These leaders connect *What* with *How*: the essence of developing good business strategy. Achieving organizational alignment is essential and instinctive for a Strategic Leader. When vision, mission, values, and strategy are aligned, constructive energy is released with enough thrust to clear obstacles. Strategic Leaders create value by assigning clear roles and responsibilities throughout the organization.

Strategic Leaders harness the power of paradigm, instinctively understanding how to leverage organizational frameworks and processes to invite the most favorable outcomes in a particular market. Such leaders design, assess, revitalize, and build it again with the goal of continuous improvement. Those with visionary traits are willing to risk integrating small increments of innovation along the way. The darker side of this leadership style are the "trust and control" issues that express themselves in autocratic decisions, outmoded policies, and tactical rigidity. But the great strength of this style is the ability to unify and empower people to achieve great things together. Building a successful and profitable enterprise is almost impossible without a Strategic Leader.

Who are the people on your team or in your organization that embody the traits of a Strategic Leader?

4. The Operational Leader

The Operational Leader achieves great satisfaction through superior execution and brings the energy of *get-it-done* to your team. When the enterprise runs like a well-oiled machine, these leaders have done their job. They are highly skilled at managing complex, interdependent systems and guiding an organization to achieve measurable results. They are excellent managers who can set benchmarks and attainable goals that will incentivize people to perform. At their best, they are honest brokers of authority and power that can be deployed throughout the organization to achieve excellent customer service.

Operational Leaders understand the need for people to fuel their operational tasks. The operation is the priority, but people are necessary. These leaders often thrive on being handed a vision and strategy so they can get to work on making it happen. It's common for Visionary Leaders to bring Operational Leaders alongside them to carry out their ideas. Strategic Leaders can help too, but strategy and vision can actually begin to compete if these leaders are not healthy enough. Operational Leaders love the challenge of actualizing and practicalizing ideas. The shadow side of this leadership style is a tendency to treat people as a means to an end. In their quest for superior execution, they may see workers as interchangeable parts of a machine. The best Operational Leaders are integrators, who can build on the talents and strengths of people and manage the relationship between all the parts and the whole.

A Visionary or Strategic Leader will almost always need an Operational Leader to be successful. All growing organizations face tensions and pains when scaling to meet and manage growth. Vision, purpose, products, processes, and services are all imperative, but without increasing the base of competent, dependable operators, the growing complexities can overwhelm the system.

Who are the people on your team or in your organization that embody the traits of an Operational Leader?

THREE CHARACTERISTICS OF A HEALTHY CULTURE

Personal Circles and Transformative Teams all have their unique place within the developmental journey of a leader. Both provide a contextual opportunity to be in transformative community with others, while supplying priceless resources for your practical decision-making as a leader in the real world of responsibilities.

As you might imagine, there are some guidelines for cultivating healthy interaction within each of these environments, so let's look at three simple but essential qualities that make them hum, compared to three qualities that can ruin their potential. Recognizing these constructive and destructive dynamics may help you better resource who and how to engage others. These qualities also make an excellent introduction to set expectations and tone for the caliber of interaction you're looking for and establishing benchmarks to guide, unify, and challenge one another.

1. Authenticity

The ability to show up with a group of peers in a secure and open fashion, willing to express the most honest and authentic version of yourself is a tremendous gift to everyone in the group. And you, as the facilitator, will set the bar for this. Your willingness to drop masks and be courageously transparent will invite others to do the same with you. You're creating a safe place together where no one has to pretend to be anything other than who they actually are right now. This personal integrity is the backbone of a Personal Circle or Transformative Team.

2. Availability

The essence of the group is a commitment to give of yourself for the benefit of others. This altruistic posture shows itself in prioritizing this set of relationships above your own needs. It looks like making every effort to be present at each gathering and available for the unexpected needs that will surface through the course of the year. It includes a physical, emotional, social, and even spiritual availability to every person in the group, starting, of course, with you.

3. Accountability

The willingness to make yourself voluntarily accountable to a group of peers is a courageous move that brings enormous rewards. As you give your Circle or Team permission to appropriately recognize areas of concern and to expect promised courses of action, you forge the tensile strength of the relationships as well as the formational potency of the group's contribution toward your success. And strict confidentiality is, of course, a must.

THREE PITFALLS IN UNHEALTHY CULTURES

In contrast to healthy culture elements, there are unhealthy elements that serve as serious pitfalls to be actively avoided. If you see these dynamics cropping up, call them out early; don't allow them to take root and choke out the very benefits you are investing all this energy to obtain.

1. Developmentally Shallow

Leaders who have not intentionally done their own development work are likely to offer contributions that only exacerbate the problems you're facing. They may offer methods and ideas that are defensive, detached, outdated, or based on idealized versions of leadership that lack authenticity. This only serves to perpetuate the cycle of dysfunction and erect roadblocks to transformative growth.

2. Emotionally Unavailable

The word-picture for this is side-by-side versus face-to-face. There is a time and place to walk, run, and even fight alongside one another, which is the side-by-side position. In unhealthy groups, however, this becomes the only way individuals are willing to connect. The fear of vulnerability and intimacy keeps these kinds of relationships from including face-to-face connections. When this happens, the collective culture becomes heavily focused on driving activity, performance, and outcomes, while neglecting meaningful connections among the group members.

3. Competitively Insecure

When leaders lack confidence in their own ability, they often default to an unconsciously competitive posture. Trying to prove their own worth—to others or themselves—their vision becomes skewed and their input compromised. You may experience them as negative or critical or overly attached to their own advice. Their need to be seen as strong and successful by the group (the Ideal Self) will inevitably highjack the agenda you're holding and sabotage the group dynamic.

In the West, we have learned to be independent rather than interdependent. Needing anything outside yourself is seen as a weakness, so we set up shields, try to do things alone, and are forced to over-function or hide the things we fail to accomplish. As humans, we can't escape being needy; we can only pretend otherwise. And we miss one of our greatest opportunities: to recognize need as a gift that creates avenues for personal growth and meaningful relationship. As we learn healthy ways to express our limitations, it invites curiosity and contributions that can synergize our leadership in powerful ways.

Your investment in a Personal Circle or the Transformative Teams framework provides parallel tracks on your leadership pathway. The embrace of a committed team of trusted colleagues offers a compounding opportunity to supercharge your potential contribution across not only your organization but also your industry.

A BETTER SAGE THAN KING

Here's how I (Jack) have experienced the Trust Circle principle in my leadership growth.

As the creator of a boutique consulting firm, my work was deeply fulfilling, even though I was dealing with the chronic issue of trading professional time for money. Occasionally, I would get anxious about my long-term financial future and resolve to build a different kind of company, developing products that might yield recurring revenue and passive income. What I didn't fully realize at the time was that building a larger, more complex company would require a level of strategic and operational leadership that I didn't naturally have. As a Soul-Starter trying to go above the line, I would either attempt to press into functions outside my strengths or recruit other inspirational people like me who struggle to build a successful business.

I learned the hard way that it is better for me to be a Sage than a King; better to fully occupy my quadrant of origin than try to make myself into another one. When I work alongside a Strategic Leader, the necessary systems and structures are built to support my vision with a synergy that works for the success of the enterprise. No business title or role exists for my lower quadrant contribution to the leadership team, so I usually call myself the Chief Strategy Officer.

I have consulted with many organizations in which the CEO is not functioning out of his or her strengths and then hired too many people out of the same quadrant. Executive leaders have a tendency to hire people they are comfortable with and who think and function the way they do, but that lack of diversity limits the capacity of the enterprise to respond to the demands of an ever-changing competitive environment. Many companies actually fail because they lack diversity of talent.

I have great strengths in coaching, counseling, and consulting that originate from the Soul, but when it comes to hardcore organizational leadership, I need a team of people who can complement my strengths, not duplicate them. Now I am very conscious of choosing strategic partners from the upper quadrants who know how to leverage my unique abilities. This is the explosive potential of the HOS as it applies to business teams and enterprises. And this may be the very key that unlocks the potential of your organization.

REFLECTION QUESTIONS

1. *How do you experience loneliness and isolation as a leader in your organization? How do you respond when you are feeling alone in your leadership roles?*

2. *Have you ever experienced a good friend or colleague cutting you off or rejecting you? What have you done to reconcile or replace that relationship in your personal or professional life?*

3. *Go ahead and brainstorm names of people who might serve you well in a Personal or Team Context:*

   - *Who offers you insight and strategy?*
   - *Who loves you for you?*
   - *Who inspires you and offers perspective?*
   - *Who fights for you?*

4. *What challenges do you anticipate in forming a Transformative Team, and what might you do to overcome them?*

6

WHERE DO WE GO FROM HERE?

Building and Installing the Apps on the OS

Four primary ingredients make us human, and this underlying truth forms the bedrock of this book. *Heart, Soul, Mind,* and *Strength*. We each have them and they resource our lives, yet we fail to intentionally develop and understand them. Some quadrants are more socially acceptable than others, but each carries its own genius that informs our becoming fully human.

When we ignore essential parts of ourselves—or those parts in others—our humanity becomes skewed. We may find ourselves a caricature of our true being—limiting our deepest contributions in leadership and in life. The HOS is a model that has worked for us as we have sought to restore more humanity in our own lives and those we serve. The HOS isn't a novel concept, nor something we've invented. It's an ancient set of truths that has been formally and informally affirmed by others throughout history.

Let's take a quick pass over the big ideas we've covered so far. In the Introduction, we looked at the opportunity within the modern leadership movement to invite those who feel like *Tin Men* in the dehumanizing aftermath of a mechanical business culture to go on a journey to recover and integrate their Heart and Soul. Then in Chapter One, we described the *intrinsic connection* between our growth and development as leaders and the development and transformation of the organization. That "polarity" can be in balance or out of balance, but one inevitably informs and shapes the other.

Chapter Two took us into the core of the HOS—the four quadrants and the four thresholds that invite us to become authentic, integrated, transformational, and ultimately, transcendent in our leadership. This chapter also invited us to move intentionally "beneath the line" to access the wisdom of Heart and Soul in our organizational roles; *this is the very crux of our message.*

In Chapter Three, we looked at how our personal starting block identifies us as a Heart-Starter, a Soul-Starter, a Mind-Starter, or a Strength-Starter and how that quadrant of origin imbues us with predictable strengths and weaknesses. Understanding these archetypes offers us the key to designing teams built upon the strategic intersection of all four giftings. We also looked at which quadrant we flow toward on our personal journey through the HOS and the unique combinations that are generated as a result.

One specific flow is called the Transformational Pathway, and this is the focus of Chapter Four. This path calls us to a lifetime of development as we embrace learning (Mind), experience (Heart), integration (Soul), and execution (Strength)—in that order—as a paradigm and practice for growth and development. We can also utilize the tools of teaching, coaching, mentoring, and training on this pathway. This can resource leaders to courageously cross the thresholds of resistance, shadow, and shame.

Chapter Five brought us to personal and professional Trust Circles as incubators for our formation as leaders. We looked at who to invite into these Circles and how to practically structure the gatherings for maximum benefit. The HOS also gives us four distinct leadership styles: the Collaborative Leader, the Visionary Leader, the Strategic Leader, and the Operational Leader, each of which brings essential talents and perspectives to a thriving enterprise.

These chapters served to illustrate and develop our five critical principles, which we'll recap here:

- Leadership growth and organizational development are interdependent.
- Leadership growth requires the integration of Heart, Soul, Mind, and Strength.
- Leadership growth is fueled by harnessing your unique design and flow.
- Leadership growth is catalyzed by a transformational pathway of change.
- Leadership growth deepens within relationships of trust.

We have obviously set these principles within the context of leadership development, but by now, you have observed that these are fundamental truths about what it means to be fully human. For us, the HOS is equally profound as a paradigm for living an effective life as it is for leading an effective organization. This paradigm also brings us to a point of decision.

COMPARING OPERATING SYSTEMS		
INDUSTRIAL OS		**THE HUMAN OS**
Power is Protected Control & Compliance is traded for the illusion of Safety & Security	POWER	**Power is Shared** Empowerment, Self-Leadership, & Collective Commitment is Prioritized
Priorities can be Organization Centric Individuals Exist to Service the Organization (Products, Processes, & Profits)	PRIORITIES	**Priorities are Mutually Affirming** Individual & Organization Exist to Mutually Affirm Deeper Meaning & Purpose
Perspectives can be Narrow Intellectual & Actionary Worldviews are Elevated	PERSPECTIVES	**Perspectives are Comprehensive** Intellectual, Actionary, Social & Mythical Worldviews are all Resourced
Contributions can be Predictably Static Leadership Contributions are Limited to Reinforcing Role-Specific Competencies	CONTRIBUTIONS	**Contributions are Systemic** Leadership Contributions Invite Personal Strengths, Passions & Uniqueness
Change can be Limited & Temporary Instruction & Inspiration is Expected to Modify Behaviors & Outcomes	CHANGE	**Change can be Transformative** Experiential Learning & Soul Intregration Deepens Lasting Outcomes
Relationships can be Competitive Elevated Independence creates Self-Promotion & Cultural Anxiety	RELATIONSHIPS	**Relationships are Mutually Supportive** Inter-Dependence Relationships of Trust Cultivate a Healthy Culture

Figure 6.1

AN ALTERNATIVE CONSCIOUSNESS

What we are really calling you to is a new way of perceiving yourself and the world around you—an encompassing frame of reference often called a *mindset.* The mindset represented by the HOS can sometimes be seen with most clarity by contrasting it with the prevailing mindset of our age: what we might call the Industrial-Mechanical Operating System that serves as the default value system across most of the western world of commerce.

Perhaps we can represent the distinctions between these two fundamental mindsets best in Figure 6.1. We are comparing and contrasting two operating systems: one that helped jump-start the industrial revolution, and the other is the HOS mindset that we believe will serve the needs of our current leadership culture. As you consider these six contrasts between the two operating systems, you may find yourself on one side in one category and on the other side in another category. Even if your industry isn't completely open or able to change in some areas, see where there might be incremental steps available to you that could unlock the powerful potential of the Human Operating System to revitalize your enterprise.

These contrasts are so critical to understand that we're going to unpack them a little further.

Power. The fundamental divide between these two operating systems comes down to radically different perspectives on power. In the Industrial-Mechanical Operating System, power is something to be preserved by a few and withheld from the many, resulting in the typical hierarchy and organizational pyramids we know so well. Power is restricted in terms of information, influence, and access with the presumption that wisdom resides in the C-suite alone. In contrast, the HOS recognizes that power is to be distributed and cultivated among the many to the benefit of the whole. This core belief allows for a culture that rewards team members for bringing their best and drawing out the best from others in an ethos that's collaborative rather than competitive. Let's look at each of the five themes represented here.

Priorities. The leadership framework within the Industrial-Mechanical OS is linear: there is a one-way flow of productivity, whereby the individual is valuable to the degree that they can prioritize and generate results for the benefit of the organization. This is an overly generalized yet broadly consistent observation. Within the HOS, however, the framework is systemic, mutually affirming and recognizing the individual in ways that value outcomes which positively impact both their organizational and personal contexts.

Perspectives. The Industrial-Mechanical approach offers a fast-track for leaders willing to work very hard to be successful in their business. Sophisticated management practices are required in the Industrial OS, but that knowledge and expertise is often depoyed towards the priorities established by industry norms and shareholder expectations. This management approach elevates efficient tangible and measuarable outcomes that can be repeated and scaled. The HOS values many of these attributes as they are essential for sustainable commerce, but our mindset is to be holistic and deepen these management practices to include the intentional growth and development of healthy leaders. In other words, how can we systematically and strategically cultivate leaders who are Authentic, Integrated, Transformational, and even Transcendent in their work?

Contributions. Under the Industrial-Mechanical mindset, leaders are usually forced to conform to the specific roles and responsibilities for which they were hired. Therefore, leader development moves exclusively toward the competencies that drive the organizational results expected for that specific position. All other giftings, unique abilities, and desires of that leader are typically dismissed or overlooked. There is systemic value in the HOS for identifying and harnessing the unique design and flow of a leader within their organization. Once leaders are more deeply considered and understood, it allows for either revising current roles, creating new roles, or redesigning the team to better align competencies with objectives.

Change. The leadership approach of the Industrial-Mechanical OS is defined by remaining "above the line," embodying the work-smarter, work-harder ethic of Mind and Strength. Threatened by anything that smacks of touchy-feely, such leaders may become annoyed and resistant to anyone challenging the status quo. They may allocate funds to leadership development as long as it complements their established perspectives and quickly translates to the bottom line. The HOS invites and supports those who embrace a holistic approach that takes knowledge "below the line" into Heart and Soul where experiential integration can take place before leading back above the line into strategic action.

Relationships. The Industrial-Mechanical culture embraces the corporate ladder. As a result, it is ruled by a scarcity mindset that remains inevitably competitive, even when masked by congeniality. Relationships in this context pose more of a threat than a resource, which means that few, if any, can be trusted. At the end of the day, you're on your own. The HOS is admittedly more idealistic. It recognizes that, even though conflict and competition are part of the human condition, we must discern and actively cultivate trustworthy relationships in ways that unlock greater potential for ourselves, our teammates, and our organizations.

We're hoping, of course, that we have made a compelling case for the organically authentic and practically rewarding attributes of the HOS. And we're hoping further that you intuitively resonate with the HOS. What we want to demonstrate as we conclude this book is the myriad of ways in which applications, or "apps" as we call them now, can be effectively built on the foundation of these core beliefs and practices.

In the following pages, we will offer three specific apps that we have built personally and observed firsthand. These are triumphs of the HOS in different spheres within the marketplace which include leaders, teams, and organizations. We hope these case studies will inspire you to build your own apps for all areas of your life and leadership now that you are embracing the values and architecture of the HOS.

EXECUTIVE LEADER INTENSIVES

Over the years, we have observed a common profile among executive leaders who want to engage in an individual leadership intensive. Because of the all-consuming nature of their work, they are often depleted to the point in which they are beyond exhaustion—their "Soul" is tired. Vacations, hobbies, and personal days no longer replenish them. These men and women feel numb because they have learned how to detach from their hearts in order to meet expectations and perform at a high level. Executive leaders often talk about feeling fragmented because of all the roles and responsibilities they carry. Rarely do they find the margin to do deep personal work and focus strategically on what is most important in their lives.

And it's not just their professional lives that suffer. Their marriages can feel one-sided as they work diligently to provide money for a great lifestyle, but do not experience much intimacy or emotional support in return. Their children are often self-absorbed and entitled, and at times, these leaders feel used instead of loved by their families.

When we dig a little deeper, there are unconscious motivations and compulsions that drive this need to achieve and be successful in business, things like festering father-wounds and abandonment issues. Underneath all of the surface issues and complexity, there is often a profound emptiness. This emptiness is hard to face because it exposes a lack of a core identity. Without a solid core, all high-performing leaders will eventually become depleted and hit the wall. They will either sabotage their life situation in some way or finally seek help for the painful isolation and vulnerability in their lives. This is the type of help we offer.

And this help is what brought Matthew to an Intensive two months ago. In this case, it was an imploding marriage that pushed him past his instinctive self-protection to engage his inner work. Both his boss and his counselor confronted Matthew with a lack of authenticity, that there was much more to be revealed of his True Self than had yet emerged. Matthew disagreed strongly; close friends had always commented on his authenticity, but deep inside, he knew it was true. He was still hiding. But the real Matthew began to come out during his one-on-one with us.

Despite his skepticism of yet another leadership event to "fix" him, Matthew opened his heart to trust the process, which included strategic journaling, safe and honest conversations, and exercises that we requested of him. What had presented as a marriage crisis was really a crisis of personal identity, and parts of him felt like an insecure, ashamed eight-year-old walking around in the body of a thirty-five-year-old. He began to see how striving to live up to this ideal version of himself ("who I think I should be") had come at a deep cost to his authenticity.

The leadership intensive was exhausting but cathartic for him, and Matthew returned to his life with new-found clarity of self along with a commitment to live more authentically from that True Self. He had looked his anger and his fear in the eye and realized that neither owns him. He could acknowledge his feelings for perhaps the first time, and he felt freshly equipped to attempt the recovery of his marriage. Time will tell the results, but what we know for sure is that Matthew is well on his way to recovering his Heart and his Soul, and that alone offers tremendous hope for his freedom.

Executive Leader Intensives are designed to address the common personal and professional issues that generate enough pain to motivate an investment in a two- or three-day transformative experience designed to strengthen the spiritual-psychological core. Much like elite athletes in their offseason, these leaders must strengthen their core because without it, they cannot perform at the highest levels. When executive leaders embrace, embody, and express their essential identity, they experience an organic flow of energy that is both sustainable and life-giving and yields ongoing transformation in their lives.

How does an Intensive work to strengthen the core? We have found that the most important place to start is with current leadership challenges. Sometimes the real leadership challenge flies under the radar, but once it is identified, then the process of working through resistance to build resilience can begin. Every leader will experience resistance to change at the edge of his or her growth, so a relationship of trust—such as a mentor, coach, or counselor—is necessary to work through that resistance and create constructive paths of change. This mentoring relationship is provided in the one-on-one Leader Intensive and continues beyond the experience itself to provide support when leaders return to their organizational context.

Before a leader arrives at the Intensive, we have her complete a personal and professional timeline. We want her to identify the turning points in her life and to describe the significance and impact of those events. Our goal is to honor the leader's story and reveal how the underlying structure of her narrative affects her performance today. Narrative reconstruction and renewal are essential to breaking self-defeating patterns and releasing new creativity and flow in a leader's life. Old scripts need to be rewritten and new ones formed so that one's life and work can be free and fulfilling.

Sometimes a leader's next essential step is best done with the tight personal focus that a Leadership Intensive offers, and sometimes the next step occurs ideally within a small community of like-minded men or women who are in a similar stage of the leadership journey. This is why our most popular HOS app at Transformed Leader is Transformative Leadership Cohorts.

TRANSFORMATIVE LEADERSHIP COHORTS

You are a unique leader with a particular set of abilities, talents, and gifts. This deep design must be understood and aligned with your sense of personal calling, stewardship, and career roles. Your life story with all of its joy, pain, and brokenness is like a beautiful work of art that must be embraced and embodied to fully express your leadership in a meaningful way.

Many in our leadership culture are longing for a stronger sense of meaning and purpose. With diminishing connection, leaders are experiencing a profound sense of alienation and loss of community. Mature leadership stands in this cultural gap and provides hope for the postmodern world of commerce. The Transformative Leadership Cohorts are an authentic experience of community that is structured to help men and women find the convergence where calling and need, design and destiny meet. At this point of convergence, leaders discover a powerful, positive influence in all of their life relationships.

The Leadership curriculum we have developed is a powerful eight-to-ten session experience for any business, sports, or nonprofit team to deepen its purpose, contribution, and connection, both professionally and personally. Some groups are comprised of a broad array of leaders from across the marketplace landscape, while others are drawn specifically from one particular organization. Our cohorts, like our individual initiatives, are designed as an application on the HOS, by which we mean that they are established upon the five principles you have learned in this book. The entire engagement functions as a macro-move through the quadrants, while every session also makes a micro-move on the Transformational Pathway.

The integration of Head and Heart is an essential element of our Cohorts. When a leader detaches or compartmentalizes the decision-making process, major mistakes and strategic errors are often the result. The very best decisions are holistic, in which Head and Heart are working in tandem to forge the wisdom, discernment, and judgment necessary for sound leadership. The Transformative Leadership Pathway of Mind to Heart to Soul to Strength is the tool for instigating integrative change processes that can have the power to create new neurological pathways and increase leadership capacity. This is truly some of our most rewarding work.

One of the more powerful experiences that leaders go through in a Cohort is an exploration of the light and dark sides of their leadership. We have worked with leaders who have gotten into serious trouble because they were unaware of their destructive potential under duress. This is where a strong core is so essential, offering executive leaders a trustworthy, dependable North Star. Core transformation provides the moral compass to integrate the light and dark sides of the Soul and prevent the unconscious compromise of one's integrity.

Janet's integrity was on the line when she walked into our last Cohort. Recounting the moment with her permission, we asked her to share her leadership challenge with the group, and the words came flying out, tumbling over one another with little coherence. She seemed detached from her words, as if she were telling a story that she was reading from a magazine.

"Janet," we interrupted. "Janet, hold up just a second. Can you tell us how you're feeling?" The disruptive invitation hung in the air. "You're saying a lot of words, explaining a ton, but you've lost us." Heads nodded in confirmation around the room. By asking for her feelings, we invited Janet out of her racing Mind and beneath the line to her Heart.

She hesitated before speaking. "I feel sad. I feel afraid." She didn't have to explain or justify; the mere acknowledgment in the room gave everyone who was present something real to connect with.

"Can you restate your leadership challenge now?" we asked.

"I've been asked to lay off twenty-five percent of my team. I know these people, care for them. I'm waking up at night filled with dread and shame over what's being asked of me. I don't know how to do this."

From there, we took Janet into her Soul, where she reconnected with her deeper desire. She remembered why she joined the company to begin with and why she believed it was changing the world in important ways. Her energy began to rise, and the whole room could feel it. Janet still believed in the mission of the company, even while acknowledging that there are hard times in the lifecycle of every organization. Difficult decisions are part of the burden of leadership, but we watched Janet begin to hold the tension more easily, more confidently. The big picture of Soul allowed her to move to Strength on the Transformational Pathway.

"So, what can you do about this Janet? What's your next step?"

Having gone under the line, her action steps were now humanized; she had faced her own humanity, as well as that of her teammates, and now she was prepared to take the courageous steps required of her. It wasn't going to be easy, but the fear and shame had lost their power over her. Janet's leadership had just taken a vital leap forward.

Executive leadership is challenging, sometimes utterly exhausting. But it doesn't have to be a grind. When leaders engage their challenges as an integral part of their transformational journey—either in an Intensive or a Cohort—their growth can be generative and liberating. The deeper work we lead individuals and teams through provides the confidence for effective life and career planning. Alignment of your vision, mission, and strategy comes much more naturally when built upon the True Self, not the Ideal or Shadow Self.

Another point of growth we observe among leaders through these events is the activation of insights for structuring leadership teams and organizational systems. When every person in an organization is functioning out of his or her strengths and empowered to lead in the right roles, the financial and social results can be truly phenomenal. We help leaders generate a personal and professional plan for the next three-to-five years, making this deeper experiential work immensely practical.

In short, integration leads to transformation, both in the lives of those we work with, as well as the full gamut of those within their circle of influence. When leaders do their inner work, their marriages and families are positively impacted, as well as their teams and organizations. We have seen this ripple-effect play out over many years with high-capacity leaders. We consider our Executive Leadership Intensives and our Transformative Leadership Cohorts to be among the most important stewardships of our professional careers, and they would be nearly impossible without the comprehensive framework of the HOS.

Cohort participant Seth Davis, CEO of The Joshua Tree Group, describes his formative journey this way: "The combination of group experiences, personal study, and deep integrative work with other marketplace leaders has produced more growth and personal transformation than any other study, coaching, or conference I've experienced. And the results are measured by increased peace in an ever-tumultuous marketplace, greater effectiveness as a leader in my business, and deeper intimacy and connectedness with my family."

Can leaders fundamentally change? Not just superficial behaviors but the critical core? We say yes. Whether the work is done one-on-one or in groups, the five core principles of the HOS contain the seeds of personal and professional transformation. Ideas don't change anyone as long as they remain merely ideas; it's when the seeds of big ideas are watered and cultivated internally by motivated individuals that the seeds of change germinate and begin to yield a harvest of truth and beauty. We could even say that the business enterprise is simply the environment in which our influence is meant to grow so that our legacy becomes authentically whole.

The next question, if we believe that we can change as individuals, is whether such change can spread to the extent that entire organizations can be transformed? We would also answer yes, although, we'll be honest: such comprehensive systemic change as this comes slowly and often painfully. Many transformational efforts are aborted when confronted by resistant power structures. And in other cases, the chain reaction of positive growth gets siloed in a department or a team that goes on to enjoy the positive benefits of the HOS within the larger dissonance of the enterprise itself

We have witnessed enough renewal among individuals and teams that we carry a bright vision for a movement throughout the business world, where the ideals and potentialities of the HOS continue to spread and transform wherever they land. We have one case study on the organizational sphere that we'd like to offer as a template for how the HOS can begin to inform and shape product development and operational flow at a systemic level.

ORGANIZATIONAL CASE STUDY

I (Rob) began to work as a strategic partner alongside Bob Westfall, founder and CEO of Westfall Gold, over six years ago. The organization launched in 2002 with a singular mission to help clients fund and resource transformational impact around the world. Bob and his team focus on the major development space and have become one of the country's premier fundraising consultancies. Their combined efforts have guided leading universities, nonprofits, and faith-based organizations in raising over *one billion dollars* for meaningful causes. Westfall Gold is an example of an organization that has organically implemented several of the core HOS principles that we've described into their operational framework, particularly as it relates to donor development.

In Bob's words, "Many nonprofit organizations treat donors in a transactional way: 'Hey, you have money. We need money. Let's put those two together and make some magic happen.' And while money is the engine for driving nonprofit altruism, if you make the story primarily about money, you compromise the relationship. Donors don't want a transactional relationship with an organization; they want to feel like they are part of making the world a truly better place. So that calls for a radically different organizational approach. That's what we're shooting for."[26]

The world has truly changed; customers are looking for more. They want great products, but they also want community; they want to feel like they have been seen and understood. Think for a moment about the difference you experience when you call a company and a human being picks up the phone. These days, that's radical. Your experience goes to a whole new level. We well know the alternative: twenty minutes of pressing buttons, navigating a complex messaging matrix of automated robots, trying to get an answer to your question. It's frustrating, exhausting, and dehumanizing.

The 2018 Fundraising Effectiveness Survey Report of the Association of Fundraising Professionals calculates that "every $100 gained in 2017 was offset by $96 in losses through gift attrition."[27] This crisis in donor attrition is a direct result of fundraising models that elevate the giving transaction over the donor relationship. By failing to take the donor below the line into Heart and Soul, such appeals prevent the donor from connecting personally with the organization's vision, and they undermine the long-term impact of the partnership. The results are poor engagement, limited giving, and low retention.

In contrast, Westfall Gold works hard to understand the language of their customers. They go to great lengths analytically, organically, and relationally to discern who their donors are and what they value. They work at the intersection of the individual and the context—a balanced polarity—in which individuals are engaged at a human level in relationship to the organizational mission. In the fundraising venue that looks like creating donor events for particular organizations in such a way that expresses their unique culture and connects human contributors to the human heart of the organization being represented.

Bob puts it this way: "There are nearly sixty-three trillion dollars' worth of wealth that will begin to transfer over the next generation. Most assumptions being made by nonprofits are that this money will simply seep into Mom and Dad's favorite charities, but this is unlikely. The next generation does not have the same giving patterns, habits, and motivations of their parents, which means that charitable organizations need to wake up and become intentionally engaged, or risk extinction."

Reflecting on Bob's point, we see great value in our own quadrant framework and worldviews of the HOS to offer an incredible resource for organizations and companies attempting to understand this new frontier. This is a time for innovation, curiosity, and creativity—all "below the line" attributes. Those who fail to engage Heart and Soul over the next decade will likely find themselves in a precarious place.

We noticed how Westfall Gold's approach to fundraising organically complements our Transformational Pathway. They essentially start by leading attendees to the Mind, where the logical case and strategic basis for support is presented, followed by a movement to the Heart quadrant, where the emotional case is then engaged. While it is common for many fundraising programs to stop here, Westfall Gold makes the defining move to take attendees into the Soul quadrant, where the transformational case for support is added.

Engaging logic and emotion are vital, but the Soul integrates the two and offers the potential donors a vantage point for how their contributions can align with an organization's vision to change and transform the lives of others. It is only at this defining point in the pathway that attendees are led back over the line into the Strength quadrant and donors are invited to make a financial commitment to support the growing impact of the organization.

As Westfall discovered, the HOS offers a standardized paradigm and language for a whole constellation of apps to be built to address numerous areas within an organization and those they serve. Companies that install the HOS are working to humanize their organization in ways that will position them for long-term success. As we noted before, not every organization will successfully install the HOS. Some will try and fail. Some will never try. And some will succeed incrementally.

An organization is a big ship to turn, and if yours is currently entrenched in transactional approaches, your customers, leaders, infrastructure, and culture will be challenged. The wisest approach is often for a leader or an executive team to catch the vision and begin to embody it in their own lives or department first; once the paradigm takes root and becomes organically formed there, then it has greater potential to inspire and catalyze a larger movement throughout the company.

We can say, however, that organizations that choose to embody the five principles of the HOS have the opportunity to set themselves apart from the current cultural leadership tides, and with that comes the hope and probability of a meaningful prosperous future. We are seeing a rise among consultants and companies seeking to install the HOS into their practices and approaches. If you are a coach or leadership consultant, this system provides a robust platform to organize and align your apps, tools, tips, and approaches. Welcome aboard.

THE NEXT STEP

Whether you sit at the helm of a Fortune 500 company, run a department of managers, or find your joy as a solopreneur, a host of opportunities await you if you're ready to install the HOS. But before you do, let's pause a moment and review the bidding.

Your current leadership perspectives, patterns, and behaviors have accumulated in a slow marinating of such formative influences as your personal experience, your memories, your culture, and the dominant leadership paradigms learned and modeled over your years. Great leaders understand that the convictions they hold in the present trace themselves far back into their early stories. Those who are willing to consider their evolution are more able to make choices that can lead to a different future. For others, autopilot and unawareness will keep them safe, and keep them in the dark. This kind of curious self-reflection holds the key to taking a new step on a new path.

We live in an impulsive, myopic culture that has abandoned the patience and process required for deep-rooted change and transformation. Western culture will predictably attempt shortcuts, but deep change is a maturing process that requires intentionality and time. Leaders who are willing to invest in their own lives at the intersection of Self and Context—the leadership environment in which they express their unique abilities —have the opportunity to change their path and to create a welcoming invitation for others to do the same.

When you do, here's what you can expect to happen: By installing the HOS, you and your leadership team will begin to transcend the Industrial-Mechanical Operating System and, in turn, you will shore-up the overall health of your organization through our five core principles. And finally, you will set an example that can inspire other leaders to make their own lifetime commitment to authentic growth and organizational transformation.

TOWARD HEART AND SOUL

Nothing could be more important for a leader's family, profession, and our culture at large than for us to make the choice to install the HOS into our lives and leadership—and, uniquely, the resources of Heart and Soul. A significant challenge these days is that most opportunities for deeper growth with others have been removed from our culture; these formative environments have been replaced with conferences and workshops that leave little space for anything beyond learning knowledge and skills alongside others, rather than engaging in transformative change in a leadership community. We are endeavoring to reverse this trend with intentional spaces, where leaders can support, encourage, and strengthen one another in Trust Circles as they engage real challenges of life.

Life has a way of bringing us to a crossroads—points of decision that will forever mark our journeys. Shakespeare famously said, "Some are born great, some achieve greatness, and some have greatness thrust upon them."[28] We believe that greatness can live quietly without drawing much attention to itself, but it will always require a choice, a certain degree of sacrifice, and a high level of commitment. Would you be willing to make this kind of commitment?

Now is the time to choose intentional steps that will deepen your Soul, integrate your Heart, and expand your influence as an emergent or mature leader. We welcome you to join us on the transformative pathway, where grace, wisdom, and love become embodied in our personal and professional lives and contexts.

Remember, deep change and transformation require that we consciously stay at the edge of our growth. This is difficult to do but costly not to. It is precisely at this point that we experience a deeper sense of our True Self and find more to offer ourselves and those around us. The world is desperately asking for leaders who are transformational, not transactional. As we said in the introduction, these types of leaders cannot be microwaved; this compelling vision calls us to the journey of a lifetime.

At Transformed Leader, we set out with one goal: to develop resources, programs, and approaches that are designed to empower leaders and organizations to grow their connection, character, capacity, and courage. And as you know now, those are the unique contributions of Heart, Soul, Mind, and Strength—the four ingredients that make us fully human.

REFLECTION QUESTIONS

1. *Is there any part of your authentic self that you are neglecting at this time? If so, how can you more fully express that latent or undeveloped part of you?*

2. *Which of the two mindsets (Mechanical-Industrial / Human OS) is most real and natural for you? What would be required of you at home and work if you shifted your mindset to the Human OS?*

3. *Looking forward, what are some positive outcomes you are desiring and hoping to experience because of the intentionality being placed on your leadership growth and development?*

4. *What is at risk for you to install the Human OS into your business or organization? How would you go about leading this kind of deep change?*

END NOTES

INTRODUCTION

1. *What's Missing in Leadership Development?* (August 17, 2017). McKinsey & Co. https://www.mcinsey.com/featured-insights/leadership/whats-missing-in-leadership-development.
2. For example, see these studies: *Why Instant Gratification is the One Marketing Tactic Companies Should Focus on Right Now.* (April 30, 2018). https://www.forbes.com/sites/jiawertz/2018/04/30/why-instant-gratification-is-the-one-marketing-tactic-companies-should-focus-on-right-now/#73845bdae91b, &
   Why Millennials Have Higher Expectations for Customer Experience than Older Generations. (March 26, 2019). https://www.forbes.com/sites/nicolemartin1/2019/03/26/why-millennials-have-higher-expectations-for-customer-experience-than-older-generations/#2664421f2ec1, and https://www.entrepreneur.com/article/235088.

CHAPTER 1

3. Johnson, B. (1996). *Polarity Management: Identifying and Managing Unsolvable Problems.* (pp. 80). HRD Press, Inc.

CHAPTER 2

4. Adapted from McWhinney, W. (1997). *Creating Paths of Change: Managing Issues and Resolving Problems in Organizations*, 31-48. Sage Publications.
5. Mandela, N. (1994). *The Long Walk to Freedom*. Back Bay Books.
6. Quinn, R. E. (1996). *Deep change: Discovering the Leader Within*, 3. Jossey Bass.

CHAPTER 3

7. Guinness, O. (1998). *The Call: Discovering the Leader Within*, 1. W Publishing Group.
8. Buechner, F. (1993). *Wishful Thinking: A Seeker's ABC*, 119. HarperOne.
9. Mark 12:30 (NIV)

CHAPTER 4

10. Glisczinski, D. J. (2011). "Lighting Up the Mind: Transforming Learning Through the Applied Scholarship of Cognitive Neuroscience." *International Journal for the Scholarship of Teaching and Learning* Vol. 5 (1), article 24, 7.

11. Mezirow, J. (1991). *Transformative Dimensions of Adult Learning*. Jossey-Bass.
12. Schults, F. L., and Sandage, S. J. (2006). *Transformative Dimensions of Adult Learning*, 31. Jossey-Bass.
13. Glisczinski, D.J. (2011), 10.
14. McCullough, D. (2005). *1776*. Simon & Schuster.

CHAPTER 5

15. *Loneliness is Bad for Our Health. Now Governments Around the World are Finally Tackling It.* (October 9, 2018). https://qz.com/1413576/loneliness-is-bad-for-our-health-now-governments-around-the-world-are-finally-tackling-the-problem/
16. *America's Loneliest Workers, According to Research*. (March 19, 2018). https://hbr.org/2018/03/americas-loneliest-workers-according-to-research
17. Bly, R. (1990). *Iron John: A Book About Men*, 34. Vintage Books.
18. Lencioni, P. (2015). *The Truth About Employee Engagement: A Fable About Addressing the Three Root Causes of Job Misery*. Jossey-Bass.
19. Greenleaf, R.K (1977). *Servant Leadership*, 64. Paulist Press.
20. Greenleaf, R.K (1977). *Servant Leadership*, 65. Paulist Press.
21. Siegel, D. (2020). *The Developing Mind: How Relationships and the Brain Interact to Shape Who We Are*, 3rd edition, 8. Guilford Press.
22. Rob Murray with Dr. Sue Johnson. (February 10, 2020). Talk of Change Podcast. Season 2, Episode 2. www.talkofchange.com
23. Zak, P. J. (2015). "Why Inspiring Stories Make Us React: The Neuroscience of Narrative." *Cerebrum*. February, 7.
24. Walch, J. (2015). "Nested Narratives: Interpersonal Neurobiology and Christian Formation." *Christian Education Journal*, Series 3,155.
25. Bakke, D. (2013). *The Decision Maker*, 202. Pear Press.

CHAPTER 6

26. Westfall, B. (2020). Rob Murray with Bob Westfall. (April 6,2020). Talk of Change Podcast, Season 2, Episode 7. www.talkofchange.com
27. Yi, R., President and COO of Westfall Gold: references 2018 fundraising.
28. Shakespeare, W. (1916). *Twelfth Night*, Act 2, Scene 5, 42. Heath and Co.

INDEX

A
Abrahams, Harold, 87
accountability, within culture, 111
achievement-oriented leaders, 38
advertising, 10
aiming, 63
Americans, mindset of, 48
anxiety, 23
Apple, 66
applications, 5, 18, 122–127
authenticity, 39, 41–42, 45, 71–72, 110–111
authentic leader of individuals threshold, 41–42
availability, within culture, 111

B
Bakke, Dennis, 107
balance, 18–21, 29
bandwidth, internal, 7
being, priority of, 27, 62–63, 68, 76
belief, 12
belonging, 53
Bly, Robert, 95–96
boredom, 28
brain, 98–100
breathing, 18
Buechner, Frederick, 53
burnout, 29
business processes, complexities of, 6

C
Capacity for Connection, 55–56. *See also* Heart

Capacity for Meaning, 57–58. *See also* Soul
Capacity for Service, 60–61. *See also* Strength
Capacity for Understanding, 58–59. *See also* Mind
Capacity to Lead, 44, 46
change
  consequences of, 87
  HOS and, 121
  Industrial-Mechanical Operating System and, 121
  leading, 23
  neurology of, 98
  operating systems and, 119
  resistance to, 23
  story and, 98–100
Character to Inspire, 41–42, 46
Chariots of Fire (film), 87
churches, structures of, 82
Churchill, Winston, 84
"Clearing the Charge," 24
coaching, 42, 81, 82–83, 103
cognitive-behavioral change, 81, 82
collaborative leadership, 105, 107
The Collective Global, 13–14
communication, resistance and, 34
community, cravings for, 11
compassion, 76
Compassion to Serve, 42–43, 46
competition, 112, 122
confidentiality, 111
conflict, 23–24
confrontation, 47
connection, 56, 98, 99–100. *See also* Heart
contributions, 119, 121
Courage to Act, 43, 46
COVID-19 pandemic, 95
creativity, fear and, 25
crossroads, decision point at, 8–10
crucible, analogy of, 79–80
culture
  accountability within, 111
  authenticity within, 110–111
  availability within, 111
  competition within, 112
  crisis of, 7–8
  defined, 22, 26
  of empowerment, 83
  healthy characteristics of, 110–111
  as impulsive, 131

languages of, 34
management of, 25–26
power within, 120
unhealthy characteristics of, 111–112
vision *versus,* 26
workplace, 96

D
Davis, Seth, 127
development, 10, 18, 21–22
doing, priority of, 27, 62, 63, 68, 76, 82
donor attrition, 129
dysfunction, 19

E
economy, purpose-driven, 11
emotion, 23, 24, 86, 112
emotional intelligence, 22–23. *See also* Mind
emotive center, Heart as, 36. *See also* Heart
empowerment, 83
emptiness, 123
encouragement, 97
executive leadership
challenges of, 126, 127
core competencies of, 21–25
dysfunction of, 96
hiring practices of, 113
intensives of, 122–124
relationships of, 122–123
experiential learning, 81, 82

F
Failure, position of, 75
fear, 25
fight, flight, or freeze, 24, 47, 85
firing, 63
flame-outs, 29
Freud, Sigmund, 36
friendship, Personal Circle and, 103
fundraising, 129–130

G
Gandalf, analogy of, 57
gift attrition, 129
Glass, Richard, 59
Glisczinski, Daniel, 80
Grace-Giver, 75
Greenleaf, Robert, 96
group conflict, 24
growth, 21, 25, 45–46, 97–98
Guinness, Os, 52

H
Head and Heart, integration of, 125
health, teams and, 23
Heart
coaching within, 82–83
as collaborative leadership, 105, 107
function of, 36
fundraising and, 130
as human reality dimension, 35
leadership challenges and, 79
as leadership threshold, 40
Mind and, 65, 69, 85–86
movement of, 64–66
Personal Circle within, 100, 101
priority of being and, 62–63
relationships and, 36, 107
resources of, 132–133
Shadow Self and, 38
Soul and, 65, 67–68, 86–87
as starter, 55–56, 61
Strength and, 64, 70
Transformational Pathway and, 79
Transformative Teams and, 105
heart-felt visionary, 65
Hitler, Adolf, 84
hitting the wall, 11–13
How question, 36, 60–61
Human Operating System (HOS)
brokenness of, 7
comparison of, 119
defined, 6
failure consequences of, 7
as growth force, 38–39
as guide, 6–7
installation of, 131–132
mindset of, 120
power of, 117
principles of, 14
Human Reality, dimensions of, 35
Human-System Polarity, 18–21, 26

I
Ideal Self, 38, 45, 76, 86
imbalance, 18–21, 27–28, 29, 63
inauthenticity, 38
individual capacity, 21
individuals

authentic leader of, 41–42
change resistance by, 23
conflict and, 24
innovation and, 24–25
legacy of, 25
as mechanical, 29–30
team role of, 22
Industrial-Mechanical Operating System, 119, 120–122
innovation, 24–25
insecurity, 17
insight, process of, 45
instant impatience, 10
integrated leader of teams threshold, 42–43
integration, 37–39, 42–43, 127
integration project, 103
intelligence, emotional, 22–23. *See also* Mind
intensives, of executive leadership, 122–124
interdependency, 112
internal bandwidth, 7
interpersonal communion, 95
interpersonal conflict, 24
isolation, 42, 57, 81, 96

J
Jesus, 36, 54
Jobs, Steve, 66
Johnson, Sue, 98
journey, metaphor of, 80

K
king, sage *versus,* 113

L
leadership. *See also* executive leadership
achievement-oriented, 38
challenges within, 79
change and, 23
choices within, 42
collaborative, 105, 107
creative-development dimension of, 67
development process of, 10, 21–22
humanizing of, 10–11
influence of, 7
need within, 117
operational, 105, 109–110
polarity and, 18–21, 29
quadrants of origin and, 54
sacrifices within, 52

servant, 42
shadow within, 86–87
strategic, 105, 108–109, 110
styles of, 33, 105
thresholds of, 40, 41–45, 84–87
transcendent, 44–45
transformational, 43
as universal polarity, 27
visionary, 105, 107–108, 110
legacy, 25, 66
Lencioni, Patrick, 96
Leonardo da Vinci, 6
Liddell, Eric, 87
liminal space, 11
loneliness, 95–96
Long Walk to Freedom (Mandela), 44
The Lord of the Rings (film), 57

M
Mandela, Nelson, 44
manipulation, 108
The Matrix (film), 84
McCullough, David, 86
McWhinney, Will, 34
meaning, 52, 53, 78
meaning center, Soul as, 37. *See also* Soul
meaning perspective, 78–79
mentoring, 42, 81, 83, 103, 124
meta-praxis, 37–39
Mind
function of, 36
fundraising and, 130
Heart and, 65, 69, 85–86
as human reality dimension, 35
leadership style of, 82
as leadership threshold, 40
movement of, 68–69
Personal Circle within, 100, 101–102
plasticity of, 98
priority of doing and, 62
Soul and, 66–67, 69
as starter, 58–59
as strategic leadership, 105, 108–109, 110
Strength and, 68, 71
teaching and, 82
Transformative Teams and, 105
mindset, 120, 122
mission statement, 6, 43, 108
motivation, 21, 42–43, 60, 123
Murphy, Troy, 27–28

mythical worldview, 35

N
narratives, power of, 99. *See also* storytelling

O
Observer, position of, 75
operating system (OS), 5–6, 119
operational leadership, 105, 109–110
organic growth, 21
organizational development, 21–22
organization(s)
authentic leaders within, 42
change within, 23
culture within, 22, 26
health within, 23
hierarchy within, 96
innovation within, 25
leadership within, 27
legacy of, 25
as mechanical, 29–30, 63
as organisms, 63
polarity and, 18–21
talent diversity within, 113
teams within, 22–23
transformational leader of, 43
outflow, unsustainable, 19
over-challenged status, 29

P
paradigm
HOS as, 34, 118, 130
learning as, 118, 131
power of, 7–8, 88, 109
passion, cravings for, 11
patience, lack of, 10
Paul, Saint, 36
peer support, 103
Personal Circle, 100, 101–104
perspective, 78, 119, 121
phoenix process, 47
pilgrimage, metaphor of, 80
Plato, 36
polarity, 18, 26–27
power, 119, 120
pride, 38, 76, 87
priorities, 119, 120–121
priority of being, 27, 62–63, 68, 76
priority of doing, 27, 62, 63, 68, 76, 82
productivity, 7, 120–121
purpose, 11, 52

purpose-driven economy, 11

Q

quadrants, HOS. *See also specific quadrants*
circuit of, 47
function of, 34
fundraising and, 130
identification within, 51–52
Image Changing-Strategic/Tactical, 62
laps through, 45–46
movement within, 64–71
of origin, 53
priorities within, 76
starting block of, 54
threshold crossing within, 84–87
Transformational Pathway within, 77–78
Transformative Teams and, 105
workplace culture and, 96
questioning, art of, 68
Quinn, Robert, 48

R

racism, 44
Ready-Aim-Fire maxim, 63
relational conflict, 24
relationships. *See also* Trust Circle
brain and, 98
decline of, 7
emotion and, 86, 112
executive leadership and, 122–123
Heart and, 36, 107
Heart-Starters and, 64
HOS and, 122
Industrial-Mechanical Operating System and, 121–122
interpersonal communion and, 95
mentoring through, 83, 103, 124
necessity of, 94
operating systems and, 119
productivity *versus,* 7
Strength-Starters and, 60
of trust, 94
workplace culture and, 96
resistance, 24, 34, 47, 85–86, 87

retreats, Personal Circle and, 103–104
rock, symbolism of, 76
The Roundtable, 102–103

S
sage, king *versus,* 113
scarcity mindset, 122
self and other, as universal polarity, 26–27
self-stewardship, 52–53
sensory worldview, 35, 36, 60. *See also* Strength
servant-leadership, 42
1776 (McCullough), 86
shadow, 86–87, 108, 109–110
Shadow Self, 38, 76
Shakespeare, William, 132
shame, 17, 38, 76, 87
Siegel, Daniel, 98
significance, finding of, 52
simplicity, 6–7
social worldview, 35
solutions, polarities and, 26
Soul
  function of, 37
  fundraising and, 130
  Heart and, 65, 67–68, 86–87
  as human reality dimension, 35
  as leadership threshold, 40
  mentoring within, 83
  Mind and, 66–67, 69
  movement of, 66–68
  Personal Circle within, 100, 101
  priority of being and, 62–63
  resources of, 132–133
  Shadow Self and, 38
  as starter, 57–58
  storytelling and, 98
  Strength and, 67, 70–71, 87
  Transformational Pathway and, 79–80
  Transformative Teams and, 105
  as visionary leadership, 105, 107–108, 110
starting block, 54
State of Being, 62
State of Doing, 62
Stinson, Brad, 13–14
storytelling, 98–100
strategic center, Mind as, 36. *See also* Mind
Strategic Expressions, 62, 63
strategic leadership, 105, 108–109, 110

Strength
function of, 36
fundraising and, 130
Heart and, 64, 70
as human reality dimension, 35
as leadership threshold, 40
Mind and, 68, 71
movement of, 70–71
as operational leadership, 105, 109–110
Personal Circle within, 100, 102
priority of doing and, 62
Soul and, 67, 70–71, 87
as starter, 60–61
training and, 82
Transformational Pathway and, 80–81
Transformative Teams and, 105

T
Tactical Expressions, 62, 63
"taking laps," 41
Tardy, Evan, 71–72
teaching, 81, 82
teams, 22–23, 42–43, 61–64, 104–106
technology, loneliness and, 95
tension, 45, 47, 79
termination, 63
thresholds, leadership, 40, 41–45, 84–87
Tin Man, analogy of, 9, 10, 117
tools of influence, 82–83
training, 81, 82
transcendent leadership, 44–45
transformation, 78–79, 127
transformational leader of an organization threshold, 43
Transformational Pathway
defined, 118
embodiment of, 83
fundraising and, 130
Heart and, 79
Mind and, 79
overview of, 77–78
purpose of, 125
Soul and, 79–80
Strength and, 80–81
Transformative Leadership Cohorts, 124–127
Transformative Teams, 104–106
transparency, 39
trauma, effects of, 93–94
True Self, 38, 42, 71–72, 76, 123

trust, 94, 99–100.
Trust Circles
change process and, 77–78
defined, 97
experiential learning and, 81
overview of, 97–98, 118
Personal Circle within, 100, 101–104
storytelling within, 99–100

U
under-challenged status, 28, 29
unitary worldview, 35
universal polarities, 26–27

V
values, 42–43
virus, Ideal Self as, 38
vision, 11, 26, 43, 57, 108
visionary leadership, 105, 107–108, 110
vulnerability, 45

W
Walch, Jason, 99
wall, hitting the, 11–13
Washington, George, 86
Westfall, Bob, 128–130
Westfall Gold, 128–132
What question, 36, 58–59
Who question, 36, 55–56
Why question, 37, 57–58, 108
willpower, 38, 80
The Wizard of Oz, 9, 10, 117

Z
Zak, Paul, 98

ABOUT THE AUTHORS

Jack Nicholson and Rob Murray are Co-founders of Transformed Leader, an innovative coaching and consulting group that helps mission-driven organizations to address and overcome their greatest leadership challenges. They are especially effective in helping leaders work through their resistance in order to develop greater connection, character, capacity, and courage as a leadership community.

Jack Nicholson

Over the past 20 years, Jack has helped growing organizations navigate the human side of executive leadership. He has coached and consulted with entrepreneurial and mid-size businesses as well as non-profit organizations to build emotionally-intelligent leadership teams and culturally-sound workplaces.

He specializes in coaching high-capacity executives in the core competencies of strategic leadership, including leading constructive change, transforming organizational conflict, building relationships of trust, and releasing creativity and innovation.

Jack has three master's degrees in Organizational Development, Counseling, and Theology and has a life-long professional interest in how transformation occurs for individuals, teams, and organizations. He is currently working on his Ph.D. in the integration of Religion and Society. He and his wife, Melissa, enjoy living on a peaceful 15-acre homestead in College Grove, Tennessee.

Rob Murray

Hailing from Cape Town, South Africa, Rob graduated from Stellenbosch University before moving to the United States in 2002. Over the last fifteen years, Rob has worked at the intersection of Faith, Business, and Social Justice. His professional journey led him to complete a Master's degree in Social & Civic Entrepreneurship, and he is currently completing a Doctorate in Transformational Leadership.

As a co-founder and CEO of *Transformed Leader*, Rob carries a deep passion for developing and facilitating transformative and experiential approaches that systemically help leaders and teams address their greatest organizational challenges. Rob is a highly effective and experienced change agent for personal and professional growth. He is the host of the *Talk of Change* Podcast.

Rob is also the President of *Westfall Speakers*, a successful talent agency that works alongside *Westfall Gold*, specializing in securing the best presenters and performers for major development campaigns and mega-donor corporate events. Rob and his wife, Natalie, along with their four beautiful children, make their home in Franklin, Tennessee.

TRANSFORMED LEADER CAN JOURNEY WITH YOU.

Reach out and connect with us to explore ways we can resource and support your transformative journey. Jack and Rob carry a deep passion for facilitating transformative and experiential approaches that can guide leaders, teams, and organizations to face and address their greatest leadership challenges.

- Leader Intensives (1-1)
- Transformative Cohorts
- Transformative Coaching
- Transformative Resources
- Experiential Workshops and Academy
- Guided Retreats (Personal or Professional)
- Emotional Resilience T-Groups
- Leadership Program Design
- Talk of Change Podcast
- Speaking... and More!

www.transformedleader.com

"TALK OF CHANGE" PODCAST

Listen in with Rob Murray on the *Talk of Change* podcast. Rob is a South African-born researcher and business leader who's fascinated with understanding and navigating deep change and transformation. In each episode he sits down with carefully selected experts, scholars, leaders, and guides opening up strong conversation that will shape your steps in finding more purpose, capacity, and connection.

www.talkofchange.com

BULK BOOK PURCHASING

Bulk book discounts are available for organizations and events looking to purchase larger quantities of *The Human Operating System* to broadly introduce these concepts to their leaders, teams, and organizations. Connect with us at Transformed Leader to inquire further.

www.transformedleader.com

Made in the USA
Thornton, CO
09/21/22 21:19:05

0a641360-6292-4c7a-a90c-778d5e908843R01